BANISH

YOUR BODY IMAGE THIEF

A COGNITIVE BEHAVIOURAL THERAPY WORKBOOK ON BUILDING POSITIVE BODY IMAGE FOR YOUNG PEOPLE

Kate Collins-Donnelly

Jessica Kingsley *Publishers*
London and Philadelphia

First published in 2014
by Jessica Kingsley Publishers
73 Collier Street
London N1 9BE, UK
and
400 Market Street, Suite 400
Philadelphia, PA 19106, USA

www.jkp.com

Library of Congress Cataloging in Publication Data
Collins-Donnelly, Kate.
  Banish your body image thief : a cognitive behavioural therapy workbook on building positive body
image for young people / Kate Collins-Donnelly.
       pages cm
  Includes bibliographical references.
  ISBN 978-1-84905-463-8 (alk. paper)
  1. Body image in adolescence--Juvenile literature. 2. Body image in children--Juvenile literature. 3.
Cognitive therapy for teenagers--Juvenile literature. 4. Cognitive therapy for children--Juvenile
literature. I. Title.
  BF724.3.B55C65 2014
  306.4'613--dc23
                                    2013044133

British Library Cataloguing in Publication Data
A CIP catalogue record for this book is available from the British Library

ISBN 978 1 84905 463 8
eISBN 978 0 85700 842 8

Printed and bound in Great Britain by Bell and Bain Ltd, Glasgow

BANISH
YOUR BODY IMAGE THIEF

by the same author

Banish Your Self-Esteem Thief
A Cognitive Behavioural Therapy Workbook
on Building Positive Self-Esteem for Young People
ISBN 978 1 84905 462 1
eISBN 978 0 85700 841 1

Starving the Anger Gremlin
A Cognitive Behavioural Therapy Workbook
on Anger Management for Young People
ISBN 978 1 84905 286 3
eISBN 978 0 85700 621 9

Starving the Anxiety Gremlin
A Cognitive Behavioural Therapy Workbook
on Anxiety Management for Young People
ISBN 978 1 84905 341 9
eISBN 978 0 85700 673 8

Starving the Stress Gremlin
A Cognitive Behavioural Therapy Workbook
on Stress Management for Young People
ISBN 978 1 84905 340 2
eISBN 978 0 85700 672 1

of related interest

Life Coaching for Kids
A Practical Manual to Coach Children and Young People
to Success, Well-being and Fulfilment
Nikki Giant
ISBN 978 1 84905 982 4
eISBN 978 0 85700 884 8

Working with Young Women
Activities for Exploring Personal, Social and Emotional Issues
2nd edition
Vanessa Rogers
ISBN 978 1 84905 095 1
eISBN 978 1 84905 095 1

Helping Children to Cope with Change, Stress and Anxiety
A Photocopiable Activities Book
Deborah M. Plummer
Illustrated by Alice Harper
ISBN 978 1 84310 960 0
eISBN 978 0 85700 366 9

Focusing and Calming Games for Children
Mindfulness Strategies and Activities to Help Children
to Relax, Concentrate and Take Control
Deborah M. Plummer
Illustrated by Jane Serrurier
ISBN 978 1 84905 143 9
eISBN 978 0 85700 344 7

CONTENTS

ACKNOWLEDGEMENTS 7

ABOUT THE AUTHOR 8

INTRODUCTION 9

1. WHAT IS BODY IMAGE? 13

2. YOUR BODY IMAGE 17

3. YOU'RE NOT ON YOUR OWN 33

4. HOW A NEGATIVE BODY IMAGE DEVELOPS: INTRODUCING THE BODY IMAGE VAULT AND THE BODY IMAGE THIEF! 43

5. HOW A NEGATIVE BODY IMAGE DEVELOPS: INFLUENCES 55

6. HOW A NEGATIVE BODY IMAGE DEVELOPS: THOUGHTS 75

7. HOW A NEGATIVE BODY IMAGE DEVELOPS: FEELINGS 85

8. HOW A NEGATIVE BODY IMAGE DEVELOPS: BEHAVIOURS 89

9. IMPACTS OF A NEGATIVE BODY IMAGE 103

10. BANISH YOUR BODY IMAGE THIEF: AN INTRODUCTION 115

11. BANISH YOUR BODY IMAGE THIEF: MANAGING YOUR THOUGHTS AND BELIEFS 127

12. BANISH YOUR BODY IMAGE THIEF: MANAGING YOUR BEHAVIOURS 169

13. BODY IMAGE DOS AND DON'TS 193

14. SUMMING UP! 199

INFORMATION FOR PARENTS AND PROFESSIONALS 223

REFERENCES 233

ACKNOWLEDGEMENTS

First, I would like to thank all the young people who have courageously shared their artwork, comments and stories in this workbook. Their aim was to help other young people to realise that they are not on their own in struggling with body image issues and to highlight that it really is possible to develop a positive body image. Thank you also to the young people, parents, practitioners and colleagues who have inspired me to develop this workbook. I would also like to thank everyone who I have worked with at Jessica Kingsley Publishers, especially my editor Caroline, for their invaluable help with my 'Starving the Gremlin' series for young people as well as for their support for this new 'Banish Your Thief' series for young people. It is always a joy to work with you. Thank you also to Tina Gothard for her fantastic Body Image Thief and Body Image Vault illustrations used throughout this workbook. Tina, it was a pleasure to work with you. And last, but by no means least, a huge thank you goes to Maria and Mark for their motivation, inspiration, support and guidance.

ABOUT THE AUTHOR

Hi! I'm Kate, and I have worked for several years providing support for children, young people and their parents on the emotional issues that children and young people face today, including body image issues. I have also provided training and guidance for professionals from a variety of disciplines on how to support children, young people and their families when a child or young person is suffering with issues such as body image disturbance. Through this work, it became evident that there was a need for a book aimed directly at children and young people on how to develop a positive body image, and as a result, *Banish Your Body Image Thief* was born.

Banish Your Body Image Thief will teach you about what body image is, how it develops, the factors that can influence it, the different ways in which a negative body image can present itself and the impacts a negative body image can have. And along the way, you will work through activities that will help you apply this knowledge to your own circumstances.

You will also learn how to build a positive body image by filling and protecting your Body Image Vault and banishing your Body Image Thief using a range of self-help strategies. Some of the young people who I have worked with have kindly contributed their stories, artwork and comments to this workbook in order to help you to see that a positive body image really is achievable!

Happy reading, and good luck banishing your Body Image Thief!

Kate

Introduction

Are you dissatisfied with the way you look?

Do you try to hide parts of your appearance?

Do you avoid going to certain places or doing certain things because of your concerns about how you look?

Do you worry that people will laugh at you or talk about you behind your back because of how you look?

Do you spend a lot of time thinking negatively about how you look?

Do you feel that you have to do certain things in order to make yourself feel better about how you look?

Do you spend a lot of time checking how you look in the mirror?

Do you judge yourself negatively as a person because of how you look?

Do you frequently seek reassurance from others about how you look?

Do you frequently compare yourself to others and believe you look worse than they do?

Do your concerns about how you look have negative impacts on you and your life?

If you have answered 'Yes' to any of the questions above, then *Banish Your Body Image Thief* is here to help you!

Banish Your Body Image Thief provides self-help tools that can be suitable for young people with varying levels of body image concerns. This workbook is based on something called cognitive behavioural therapy (CBT) and something called mindfulness.

CBT is where a therapist helps people to deal with a wide range of emotional problems, including body image concerns, by looking at the links between how we THINK (our cognition), how we FEEL (our physical feelings and emotions) and how we ACT (our behaviour).

think   feel   act

Mindfulness originates from the spiritual discipline of Buddhism and from meditation and yoga practices. When we practise mindfulness we make a choice to:

- become AWARE of our thoughts and feelings in the here and now

- ACCEPT our thoughts and feelings as they are, without criticising or judging them or ourselves or viewing them as reality

- LET negative thoughts and feelings GO instead of focusing on them over and over and over again.

As you progress through this workbook, you will complete activities that will teach you about CBT and mindfulness in order to help you banish your Body Image Thief and improve your body image.

Because body image concerns come in many different shapes and sizes just as our bodies do and because there are many different strategies that can help people to overcome their body image concerns, I couldn't put this book together in a few pages! But please don't let the length of this workbook put you off completing it! Working through this book as a whole will provide you with the fullest knowledge and the most opportunities to practise what you have learnt through a variety of activities. However, if you want to make a quick start or feel that certain parts aren't as relevant to you as others, then please feel free to dip in and out of the parts that are most important to you. But don't forget that you can always return to the full book at any time in the future.

For some young people, this workbook may not be the only help they will need. Sometimes, self-help tools alone are not sufficient to help a person to make all the changes and improvements that they need to. In some cases, it is important for a person to seek treatment from a mental health professional, such as a psychologist, psychiatrist, counsellor or therapist – for example, if a person's body image concerns are severe and/or accompanied by other mental health disorders, such as eating disorders, body dysmorphic disorder (BDD) or depression, or negative coping strategies, such as substance abuse or self-harming (which we will explore in Chapter 9). If this is the case, this workbook is suitable to be used alongside such professional treatment. Also, please note that you may need to talk to someone you can trust such as a parent, relative, friend, teacher or counsellor if working through this book raises difficult issues for you.

So now that you have learnt about this workbook, its purpose, its basis and who it is suitable for, let's get started on banishing your Body Image Thief and overcoming your body image concerns!

1

What is
Body Image?

Step 1 of improving your body image is to understand what body image is. Now although this is really important, I don't need to spend pages and pages explaining it. Let's keep it simple. Your body image is...

**how you think and feel about your body
or your appearance or your looks.**

Here are some examples of thoughts and feelings that other young people have about their bodies.

'I'm so spotty it's horrible! I'm so ashamed.' (Fran, 14)

'I'm not perfect, but hey, who is? I'm just me and that's OK!' (Sally, 12)

'I'll never get a girlfriend unless I lose weight!' (Karl, 16)

'I hate my body. All of it!' (George, 11)

'I can't wait until I'm old enough to make my own decisions about my hair. The moment I am, I'm getting rid of the ginger ugliness that sits on my head. I'm dyeing it blonde. After all, every guy loves a blonde!' (Vicky, 13)

'I don't care what anyone else says or thinks about how I look! I'm happy with myself. That's what counts.' (Clive, 14)

'So I'm never going to be blonde, tall, skinny and leggy and get drooled over like Melanie in my year at school. But I know it's who you are as a person that's important!' (Kristen, 12)

'I can't help being thin, but all the adults think I'm anorexic, all the girls at school hate me and the boys laugh at me for being flat chested. I hate how I look!' (Lily, 16)

These thoughts and feelings can also impact on how people behave and on their lives in general. Here are the same young people describing how they act in response to their thoughts and feelings about their bodies.

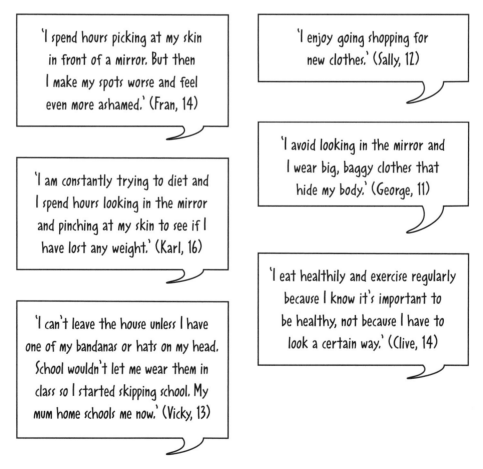

'I started self-harming two years ago to try and cope with the comments people make about me.' (Lily, 16)

'I just ignore the comments other girls at school make about my height and my glasses!' (Kristen, 12)

'I try on so many different outfits before I go out to play with my friends after school and I constantly ask my mum if I look OK.' (Roisin, 10)

'I bully other people about how they look so I don't get bullied back.' (Marlon, 15)

'I spend hours every evening on my gym equipment at home and have started stealing my older brother's protein shakes.' (Ollie, 15)

Some of the young people above have a positive body image and some of them have a negative body image. You will learn more about the links between our thoughts, feelings and behaviours and how these links help to determine whether we have a positive or a negative body image as you progress through this workbook, as understanding this is key to improving your body image.

think   feel   act

But first you need to assess exactly how you think and feel about your body at this point in time and what impacts these thoughts and feelings are having on your behaviours and on your life in general. This is Step 2 in improving your body image. There is a questionnaire in the next chapter to help you to do this.

2

Your Body Image

When we have body image concerns, we can sometimes try to hide or disguise or camouflage parts of our bodies in some way. We can also try and hide our body image concerns from other people too, as well as from ourselves, because acknowledging them can seem too painful. But hiding our problems does not help us to overcome them.

So I'm asking you to be brave. I'm asking you to put the mask that you may have been hiding behind down and think honestly about how you respond to your body and the impact this has on you by completing the following questionnaire. Before we can ever address any problem, we have to acknowledge that the problem is there.

MY BODY IMAGE QUESTIONNAIRE

1. **How happy are you with your overall appearance? Tick which answer applies to you.**

   a) Very happy ☐   c) Mostly unhappy ☐

   b) Mostly happy ☐   d) Very unhappy ☐

2. **Do you worry a lot about your appearance? Tick which answer applies to you.**

   a) Yes ☐   b) No ☐

3. **At what age did you start to worry about your appearance? Tick which answer applies to you.**

   a) 0–5 years old ☐   c) 11–15 years old ☐

   b) 6–10 years old ☐   d) 16–18 years old ☐

4. **Do you wish that you could worry about your appearance less? Tick which answer applies to you.**

   a) Yes ☐   b) No ☐

5. **How different is how you look from how you would like to look? Tick which answer applies to you.**

   a) Completely different ☐   c) A little different ☐

   b) Quite a bit different ☐   d) No difference ☐

6. **Dotted around the skeleton below are different physical characteristics. Please colour in or highlight any that relate to parts of your body that you dislike. Then circle the ones that are causing you most concern, distress or worry at the moment.**

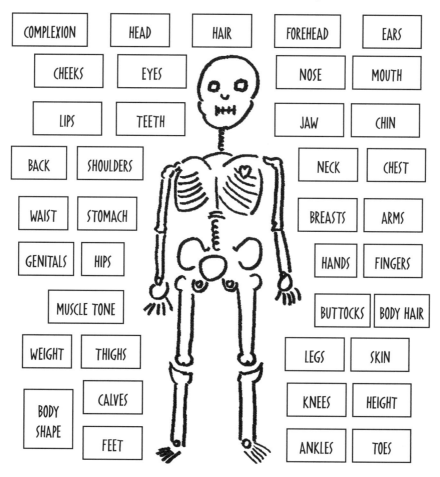

COMPLEXION HEAD HAIR FOREHEAD EARS

CHEEKS EYES NOSE MOUTH

LIPS TEETH JAW CHIN

BACK SHOULDERS NECK CHEST

WAIST STOMACH BREASTS ARMS

GENITALS HIPS HANDS FINGERS

MUSCLE TONE BUTTOCKS BODY HAIR

WEIGHT THIGHS LEGS SKIN

BODY SHAPE CALVES KNEES HEIGHT

FEET ANKLES TOES

7. **If there are other physical characteristics that cause you concern, distress or worry which aren't listed above, please write them down below.**

    ....
    ....
    ....
    ....

8. **From your answers to questions 4 and 5, pick the parts of your physical appearance that cause you the most concern, distress or worry and write down below why you don't like them.**

    ....
    ....
    ....
    ....

9. **How noticeable do you think the physical characteristics that you don't like are to other people? Tick which answer applies to you.**

    a) Not at all   ☐   d) Very   ☐

    b) Slightly   ☐   e) Extremely   ☐

    c) Moderately   ☐

10. **How much time do you spend thinking about your appearance each day? Tick which answer applies to you.**

    a) Less than an hour per day   ☐

    b) 1 to 3 hours per day   ☐

    c) More than 3 hours and less than 8 hours a day   ☐

    d) More than 8 hours per day   ☐

11. In the table below is a list of different types of appearance-related thoughts that people can have. Please indicate in the table how often you have these types of thoughts.

TYPE OF THOUGHT	HOW OFTEN I HAVE THAT TYPE OF THOUGHT				
	VERY OFTEN	OFTEN	SOMETIMES	RARELY	NEVER
Other people treat me differently because of my appearance					
Other people think I am unattractive					
Other people stare at me, talk about me or laugh at me because of my appearance					
The first thing that people notice about me is what's wrong with my appearance					
I am unattractive					
I dislike the way I look					
If my appearance is not attractive enough, then I am a worthless person					
If my appearance is not attractive enough, then I will have no friends					

TYPE OF THOUGHT	HOW OFTEN I HAVE THAT TYPE OF THOUGHT				
	VERY OFTEN	OFTEN	SOMETIMES	RARELY	NEVER
If my appearance is not attractive enough, no-one will ever love me					
I must look perfect					
My appearance is an important part of who I am					
My appearance is more important in life than other things about me					
If I looked better, I would be happier					
If I looked better, my life would be better					
My appearance has ruined my life					
No-one will ever like me unless I change how I look					
I need to radically change how I look					
How you look on the outside is a sign of who you are on the inside					
Everyone else of a similar age to me looks better than me					

TYPE OF THOUGHT	HOW OFTEN I HAVE THAT TYPE OF THOUGHT				
	VERY OFTEN	OFTEN	SOMETIMES	RARELY	NEVER
If I didn't hide or camouflage how I really look, people wouldn't like me					
I have to look perfect for people to like me					
I will never look as attractive as others					
If my appearance is flawed, then I can't be attractive					
The only way to feel better is to change how I look					
I need to be thin to be attractive					
I need to be curvy to be attractive					
I need to be muscular to be attractive					
There is nothing I can do to look good					
People are only trying to make me feel better when they pay me compliments					

12. Do you regularly avoid any of the following because of your appearance? Highlight or colour in any that apply to you.

PUBLIC PLACES	SOCIAL SITUATIONS	BUYING NEW CLOTHES
LOOKING IN THE MIRROR OR OTHER REFLECTIVE SURFACES	PHYSICAL ACTIVITIES/SPORTS	PHYSICAL CONTACT WITH OTHERS
LOOKING AT YOURSELF WHEN UNDRESSED	DRESSING OR UNDRESSING IN FRONT OF OTHERS	HAVING YOUR PHOTOGRAPH TAKEN
BEING SEEN WITHOUT MAKE-UP	BEING SEEN IN BRIGHT LIGHTING OR FROM CERTAIN ANGLES	TRYING ON NEW CLOTHES AT THE SHOP
CONVERSATIONS ABOUT PHYSICAL APPEARANCE	BEING NEAR PEOPLE YOU THINK ARE ATTRACTIVE	LETTING PEOPLE SEE THE PARTS OF YOUR BODY YOU DISLIKE
OPPORTUNITIES FOR OTHER PEOPLE TO COMMENT ON YOUR APPEARANCE	OTHER BODY OR APPEARANCE-FOCUSED ACTIVITIES	

13. Do you regularly use any of the following in order to 'hide' your appearance in some way? Highlight or colour in any that apply to you.

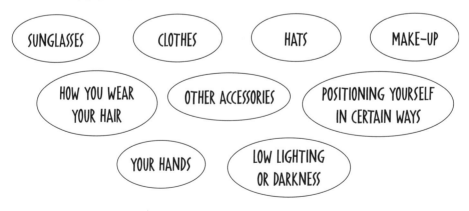

SUNGLASSES   CLOTHES   HATS   MAKE-UP

HOW YOU WEAR YOUR HAIR   OTHER ACCESSORIES   POSITIONING YOURSELF IN CERTAIN WAYS

YOUR HANDS   LOW LIGHTING OR DARKNESS

14. Do you do any of the following in order to try to 'fix' your appearance in some way? Highlight or colour in any that apply to you.

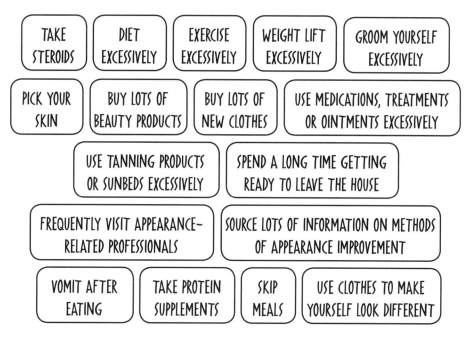

TAKE STEROIDS

DIET EXCESSIVELY

EXERCISE EXCESSIVELY

WEIGHT LIFT EXCESSIVELY

GROOM YOURSELF EXCESSIVELY

PICK YOUR SKIN

BUY LOTS OF BEAUTY PRODUCTS

BUY LOTS OF NEW CLOTHES

USE MEDICATIONS, TREATMENTS OR OINTMENTS EXCESSIVELY

USE TANNING PRODUCTS OR SUNBEDS EXCESSIVELY

SPEND A LONG TIME GETTING READY TO LEAVE THE HOUSE

FREQUENTLY VISIT APPEARANCE-RELATED PROFESSIONALS

SOURCE LOTS OF INFORMATION ON METHODS OF APPEARANCE IMPROVEMENT

VOMIT AFTER EATING

TAKE PROTEIN SUPPLEMENTS

SKIP MEALS

USE CLOTHES TO MAKE YOURSELF LOOK DIFFERENT

15. Have you ever had or thought about having cosmetic surgery or treatment because of your concerns about your appearance? Tick which answer applies to you.

a) Yes ☐   b) No ☐

16. Do you regularly do any of the following in order to 'check' your appearance in some way? Highlight or colour in any that apply to you.

SEEK REASSURANCE ABOUT HOW YOU LOOK FROM OTHERS

COMPARE YOURSELF TO OTHERS

CHECK YOUR APPEARANCE IN THE MIRROR

MEASURE PARTS OF YOUR BODY

CHECK YOUR BODY THROUGH TOUCHING, POKING, PRODDING, SQUEEZING, PINCHING AND PICKING

17. Do your appearance-related thoughts and behaviours cause you to feel any of the following? Highlight or colour in any that apply to you.

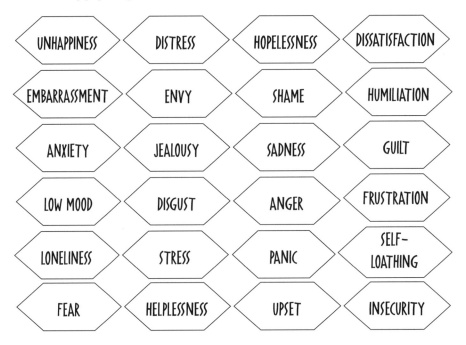

UNHAPPINESS   DISTRESS   HOPELESSNESS   DISSATISFACTION

EMBARRASSMENT   ENVY   SHAME   HUMILIATION

ANXIETY   JEALOUSY   SADNESS   GUILT

LOW MOOD   DISGUST   ANGER   FRUSTRATION

LONELINESS   STRESS   PANIC   SELF-LOATHING

FEAR   HELPLESSNESS   UPSET   INSECURITY

18. Has your body image had negative effects on any of the following aspects of your life? Highlight or colour in any that apply to you.

Physical health   Mental health and emotional wellbeing   Family relationships   Friendships

Performance at school/college/work/leisure activities   Motivation to do things   Romantic relationships

19. Do you believe changing your body image is in or out of your control? Tick which answer applies to you.

a) In my control   ☐   b) Out of my control   ☐

Now have a go at another activity that can help you to understand some more about your body image. In the next Body Image Box, try showing how you think and feel about your body and how you act as a result through one of the following creative methods:

- Draw a picture.
- Write a song or rap.
- Write a poem.
- Write a short story or play.
- Write a blog.
- Take a photo or series of photos.
- Draw or write down ideas for a short film.
- Draw or write down ideas for a dance piece.

To inspire you, you'll find a poem called 'A Perfect World Full of Perfect Girls' written by Joanne, aged 13 years, a rap called 'Some Kind of Dysmorphia' written by Dave, aged 16 years, and some pictures created by other young people on the pages that follow.

BODY IMAGE BOX

Let's get creative

A PERFECT WORLD FULL OF PERFECT GIRLS

The world is full of perfect girls
Thin, slim, beautiful and tall
Each and every one of them
Seems to have it all

The world is full of perfect bodies
Thin, slim, beautiful and lean
Each and every one of them
Seems to be a queen

The world is full of perfect girls
With their perfect lives
Whilst I live in my body pit
Struggling to survive

The world is full of perfect girls
Did I mention that they are tall, beautiful and slim?
And on their arms are their perfect boyfriends
Whilst I live alone in my body grim

Where is my perfect world?
Surely it should also be mine to gain
All I ask for is for my body to be perfect
So that I no longer have to live in such pain
By Joanne, aged 13 years

By Florence, aged 15 years

By Neela, aged 14 years

SOME KIND OF DYSMORPHIA

Oh yeh, muscle dysmorphia
That's what the shrink tells me it is

She tells me I'm obsessed
With wanting my pecs and arms to look their best

But all I want is to look like a man
Like Van Diesel and Jean-Claude Van Damme

What's so wrong with that?
It's better than being the current me which is fat

I lift weights for hours every night
But she tells me that's not right

She talks about the dangers of steroids
And how they're not good for teenage boys

But what she doesn't understand
Is that I need to feel like a proper man
By Dave, aged 16 years

By Luke, aged 11 years

And here's a final method for helping you to become more aware of your body image...

My Body Image Diary.

Completing this diary on occasions will help you to become more aware of how you think and feel about your body and what behaviours and impacts this leads to.

MY BODY IMAGE DIARY

Date ....

The situation

....

What was I thinking?

....
....

How was I feeling?

....
....

How did I behave?

....
....

What were the impacts?

....
....

Your body image can be classed as negative if your answers to the My Body Image Questionnaire and My Body Image Diary revealed that you:

- frequently THINK in negative or unrealistic ways about your body
- frequently FEEL negatively about your body
- frequently ACT in self-defeating ways, such as avoiding situations, hiding parts of your body, and checking and trying to fix your appearance
- have experienced negative IMPACTS in your life as a result

...and if your drawing, song, rap, poem, short story, play, blog, photos, short film or dance piece showed the same thing. But please don't worry if this is the case. You're not on your own in feeling this way, as the following chapter will show.

You're Not on Your Own

Step 3 in improving your body image is realising that you are not on your own in experiencing body image issues. Researchers have asked children and young people across the world about their body image through face-to-face interviews and online and paper-based surveys. And the findings are clearly showing that body image is a real concern for children and young people. More research has been conducted on female body image than male body image so far. However, this is thankfully beginning to change. I can't show you all the research that is available as that  would be a book in itself! But I'm going to show you some examples. And what is clear from these examples is that you are not on your own in worrying about your appearance. Let's see why by reading *The Body Image Times*.

THE BODY IMAGE TIMES

DOES AGE MATTER?

Studies highlight that teenagers in particular are vulnerable to developing a negative body image. For example, a 2012 inquiry by the Children's Society found that body image concerns increased with age. Twenty-five per cent of the 10–11-year-olds studied often worried about their appearance. But this increased to 37 per cent for 12–13-year-olds and 42 per cent for 14–15-year-olds.

Research is also showing that more and more young children are developing body image concerns too. For example, a 2006 study by Birbeck and Drummond reported that girls as young as 6 are expressing concerns about their weight and body shape. A study in 2000 by Schur, Sanders and Steiner found that some 6-year-olds see their bodies as larger than they actually are. And a 2006 study by Dohnt and Tiggemann reported that some girls are becoming aware of beauty ideals and dieting methods between 5 and 8 years of age.

The Body Image Times, Page 1

IT'S NOT JUST A GIRL THING!

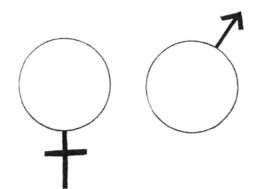

It is time to dispel the myth that body image issues only affect girls! Research is highlighting how body image issues in young males are very much on the increase. For example, a survey of over 150,000 children in 2008 by Ofsted found that, by the age of 10, a third of girls and 22 per cent of boys cited their bodies as their main source of worry.

But as you will see there is a key difference between boys and girls when it comes to body image. Although boys are concerned with weight too, they are more focused than girls on muscle mass and tone. For example, a 2011 World Health Organization study found that boys were more likely to report being too thin and girls being too overweight. A 2011 research study by Ricciardelli *et al.* also found that 25 per cent of girls aged between 8 and 11 years old compared their weight to their peers and 26 per cent of boys of the same age compared their muscles. And a survey by *Bliss Magazine* in 2004 found that 6 out of 10 girls surveyed thought that they would be happier if they were thinner.

The Body Image Times, Page 2

HOW DOES A NEGATIVE BODY IMAGE SHOW ITSELF IN YOUNG PEOPLE?

Research has also looked at the different ways that young people with body image issues feel like they have to behave due to their thoughts and feelings about their bodies, and the impact that their body image issues can have on their lives.

For example, research by the beauty company Dove (Etcoff *et al.* 2006) found that 97 per cent of the 1000 15–17-year-old girls studied believed that changing some aspect of themselves would make them feel better.

A 2011 survey conducted by the Centre for Appearance Research and the Central YMCA of 810 young people and 759 adults found that 34 per cent of adolescent boys and 49 per cent of adolescent girls had been on a diet to change their body shape or to lose weight. Also, 1 in 5 young men had used protein supplements to try and become more muscular.

A survey by *Bliss Magazine* in 2004 found that more than a quarter of the 14-year-old girls surveyed had considered having plastic surgery or taking diet pills.

A 2011 research study by the ACMD (Advisory Council on the Misuse of Drugs) showed steroid usage to be on the increase in male teenagers in the UK.

A 2005 research study by Neumark-Sztainer found that over one half of the teenage girls and nearly one third of the teenage boys studied used unhealthy weight control behaviours such as skipping meals, fasting, smoking cigarettes, vomiting and taking laxatives.

A 2010 research study by the beauty company Dove found that over 60 per cent of the girls surveyed avoided certain activities as a result of their body worries. Examples of avoided activities included going to the beach or pool, trying out for a team or club, going to a social event, party or club, going to school and voicing an opinion.

A survey of 25,000 people by BBC Radio 1's Newsbeat and 1Xtra's TXU in 2007 found that more than half of the female respondents aged between 12 and 16 years believed that their body image stops them from getting a boyfriend or relaxing in a relationship.

The Body Image Times, Page 3

BODY IMAGE AROUND THE WORLD

Body image issues are international jetsetters! They affect young people across the globe.

For example, a 2012 study of 138 young people from Northern Ireland aged 12 to 18 years found that 33 per cent were either not very happy or not at all happy with their appearance (Young NCB NI Advisory Group and NCB NI Staff 2012).

A survey of over 2000 young people aged 10 to 21 years in the Republic of Ireland found that 43 per cent were dissatisfied with their body image (O'Connell and Martin 2012).

The National Survey of Young Australians in 2010 found that body image was the most important area of personal concern for young people (Mission Australia 2010).

In the 2007 Victoria University of Wellington's Youth Connectedness Survey of young people in New Zealand, approximately 11 per cent of those surveyed were unhappy with their looks and approximately 18 per cent were unhappy with their weight in particular.

And in a 2012 study by Eisenberg, Wall and Neumark-Sztainer of American males aged approximately 11 to 18 years, more than 40 per cent regularly exercised with the goal of increasing muscle mass, 38 per cent had used protein supplements and nearly 6 per cent had used steroids.

The Body Image Times, Page 4

IT'S NOT JUST YOUNG PEOPLE WHO ARE AFFECTED!

Research clearly shows that body image issues affect adults of both genders, not just children and young people. For example, a 2012 survey by the Centre for Appearance Research found that 60 per cent of adults feel ashamed about the way they look. And a large-scale inquiry into body image in the UK reported that more than half of the UK population is dealing with mental and physical problems relating to a negative body image (APPG 2012).

Regarding men in particular, a 2011 study by the YMCA, the Centre for Appearance Research and the Succeed Foundation found the following:

- Approximately 38 per cent of the men studied would trade at least one year of their life to achieve their ideal body weight and shape.

- Approximately 78 per cent wished they were more muscular.

- At any one time, approximately 32 per cent of men use protein shakes and supplements and 18 per cent are on a high-protein diet in an attempt to build muscle mass, and 16 per cent are on a calorie-controlled diet in an attempt to slim down.

- Fifteen per cent would consider taking steroids.

- Approximately 32 per cent had exercised in a 'driven or compulsive way', 4 per cent had made themselves vomit and approximately 3 per cent had used laxatives in an attempt to control their weight.

Regarding women, a survey by *Grazia Magazine* in 2006 found that 98 per cent of British women dislike their bodies and that the average woman worries about her body every 15 minutes. A MORI poll for International Women's Day in 2012 found that 50 per cent of women feel under pressure to look good at all times and 46 per cent of women feel under pressure to lose weight. And research by the beauty company Dove (Etcoff *et al.* 2006) found that 9 out of 10 of the 2300 women studied across 10 countries wanted to change some aspect of their appearance.

The Body Image Times, Page 5

WHAT DO YOUR TEACHERS THINK?

Research also shows that teachers are concerned about the extent of body image issues in children and young people today. For example, the Association of Teachers and Lecturers in the UK conducted a survey of teachers and lecturers in 2013. The teachers and lecturers surveyed felt the following:

- Both boys and girls experience anxiety due to body image issues.

- Girls were more likely to go on a diet while boys were more likely to excessively exercise.

- Some girls use clothes to disguise their body.

- Some boys use protein shakes to improve their physique.

- Girls were striving to meet unrealistic beauty ideals.

- Some students develop eating disorders in an effort to live up to the perfect body image.

- The media put the biggest pressure on both sexes to have the 'perfect' body through TV shows and gossip magazines, followed by peer pressure.

- The pressure on young people to achieve a particular body image is increasing due to social media, celebrity magazines and television shows that promote perfect bodies.

- Their students experience abusive comments about their appearance on social networking sites.

The Body Image Times, Page 6

WHAT DO POLITICIANS THINK?

MPs in Britain were surveyed about body image and 40 per cent of the 150 MPs believed that there should be compulsory lessons on body image in schools (YMCA 2011).

They also felt that the three sectors of society who are responsible for contributing to negative body image among the British public are celebrity culture, the fashion industry and advertisers.

The Body Image Times, Page 7

If you could have your say on what is needed to address body image issues in young people today, what would you tell the politicians? Write a letter to your government with your suggestions in the next Body Image Box. If you would like to, produce a copy of this letter and send it to your local politician.

BODY IMAGE BOX

My letter to a politician

Hopefully by now you realise that you're not on your own in experiencing body image issues. This is really important to remember. But it's also really important to remember that your body image can change and it can be improved. And many people have managed to achieve this. So let's move on to Step 4 in improving your body image, namely understanding how a negative body image can develop.

How a Negative Body Image Develops

Introducing the Body Image Vault and the Body Image Thief!

Think, feel, act!

think   feel   act

Cognitive behavioural therapy (CBT) teaches us that it is how we THINK about TRIGGERS (such as situations, experiences, interactions, people, places and things) that leads to how we FEEL and to how we then ACT, as the model below shows.

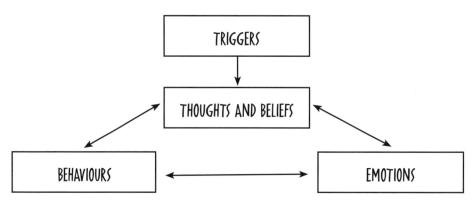

So this teaches us that it is how we THINK about our bodies that leads us to FEEL a certain way about our bodies, which in turn leads us to ACT in certain ways. We need to bear this process in mind as we now look at how our body image can develop and change over time and why it can become negative. To start us off, let me introduce you to the Body Image Vault.

The Body Image Vault

Let's imagine that we each have a special place in which we store our body image – that is, our thoughts and feelings about our bodies. That special place is your...

Body Image Vault.

Everyone's Body Image Vault has a range of special features.

SPECIAL FEATURE NUMBER 1: IT'S NEVER-ENDING!

It can keep expanding on the inside to take as many thoughts and feelings about our bodies as we like! Unlike your average vault, it will never run out of storage space!

SPECIAL FEATURE NUMBER 2: ITS DEFENCE SYSTEM

Every vault needs a defence system to protect the valuables that are being stored inside it, and the Body Image Vault is no exception. But the difference between a standard vault and the Body Image Vault is that the Body Image Vault's defence system is linked to its owner's behaviour!

SPECIAL FEATURE NUMBER 3: ITS THOUGHTS AND FEELINGS DUMP!

It has a dark, dusty, cobwebby corner right at the very back in which you can dump any thoughts and feelings that you no longer want to keep! You'll learn more about this special feature in Chapter 10.

When we are young!

As very young children, when we think and talk about our appearance, it tends to be based on facts, such as:

But with each passing day, month and year, we go through more and more experiences in life and spend more and more time with other people. And the older we get, the more varied these experiences get and the greater number of people we interact with. All of these experiences and interactions have the potential to INFLUENCE how we think and feel about our bodies (i.e. our body image). But why is this?

Because it is from these experiences and interactions that we start to learn things about our bodies, as well as how other people view our bodies, and what kinds of body types are depicted as 'ideal' by certain people in our lives and in society as a whole.

We then respond to these situations and interactions through our THOUGHTS, FEELINGS and BEHAVIOURS. Depending on the nature of these thoughts, we will either FEEL positively or negatively towards our bodies. It is these kinds of thoughts and feelings that we store in our BODY IMAGE VAULT and that determine whether OUR BODY IMAGE IS POSITIVE OR NEGATIVE.

Positive body image

If our Body Image Vault gets filled with:

- thoughts about our bodies and the importance of appearance that are based on facts ('REALISTIC THOUGHTS')

- thoughts that show we are accepting of our bodies just as they are ('ACCEPTING THOUGHTS')

- feelings in response to our bodies that show we approve of our bodies ('POSITIVE FEELINGS')

...our body image will be positive.

And the Body Image Vault wants to protect these realistic, accepting and positive thoughts and feelings for us to help our body image remain positive. And it does this using its SPECIAL FEATURE NUMBER 2 – ITS DEFENCE SYSTEM. But, as I said, how well our Vault's defence system works depends on how we ACT.

In order for it to have the most high-tech and effective defence system available, our Body Image Vault needs us to act in ways that are constructive. Constructive behaviours add locks, bolts, chains and security lights to our Vault. And the more locks, bolts, chains and security lights our Vault has, the better protected our thoughts and feelings are.

...and our body image can remain positive as a result!

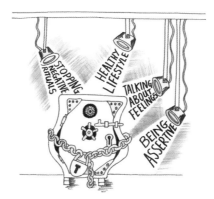

Here's one young child's story as an example.

CHRIS'S STORY

Chris, aged 4, thinks thoughts such as 'I have a birthmark on my face and that's OK'. He feels positive about his body, and is able to tell a parent or teacher when someone says something nasty about his birthmark and then quickly forget about it. Chris's Body Image Vault is full of realistic and accepting thoughts and positive feelings about his body and it is well protected due to his constructive behaviours.

Negative body image

But not everyone thinks and feels positively about their bodies all of the time. Some people will find that certain life experiences they go through and things that certain people say about them make it more difficult for them to think in realistic and accepting and positive ways about their bodies at certain times – that is, these situations have a NEGATIVE INFLUENCE on them. Thus, some people may start to THINK IN OVERLY NEGATIVE AND UNREALISTIC WAYS about their bodies at those times. This can then lead to these people FEELING NEGATIVELY towards their bodies too. And these thoughts and feelings will start to gather in their ever-expanding Body Image Vaults alongside any realistic, accepting and positive thoughts and feelings they may have.

As people start to accumulate more and more of these negative thoughts and feelings in their Body Image Vaults, they are also more likely to start ACTING IN SELF-DEFEATING WAYS in response to those negative thoughts and feelings. The result is that their Vault's defence system starts to break down gradually over time...

- Chains begin to snap and fall off.
- Old-fashioned locks break and fall off.
- High-tech digital locks get viruses and open.
- The bulbs blow in the security lights and eventually the lights smash to the ground.

We will look at the different types of influences, thoughts, feelings and behaviours that can lead a Body Image Vault's defence system to break down in detail in Chapters 5 to 8, but for now, let's see what happened to Chris as he got older for some examples.

CHRIS'S STORY CONTINUED

At the age of 10, Chris starts to get bullied about his birthmark. After a while he can't get negative thoughts about his birthmark out of his head. He begins to avoid looking in the mirror as his birthmark disgusts him. He starts to believe that it makes him unattractive. He starts to use make-up to try and hide it. Chris's Body Image Vault begins to get clogged up with negative and unrealistic thoughts and feelings and its defence system begins to fall apart.

So if a Body Image Vault's defence system breaks down like Chris's has, it means that the Vault is vulnerable. And the character it is vulnerable to is...

the Body Image Thief!

The Body Image Thief

The Body Image Thief isn't the nicest character you'll ever meet. He thinks only about himself and doesn't have any morals! In fact, he makes his living out of stealing other people's positive body image!

He wants you to be negatively influenced by experiences and interactions in life. He wants you to fill your Body Image Vault with negative thoughts and feelings. He wants you to act in self-defeating ways so your Vault's defence system breaks down.

And when that happens, he will be waiting and ready to creep into your Vault and STEAL ANY POSITIVE, ACCEPTING AND REALISTIC THOUGHTS you have in there...

...and LEAVE THE NEGATIVE AND UNREALISTIC ONES BEHIND!

The result is...

negative body image

and

negative impacts on you and your life.

And the more negative impacts your negative body image has on you and your life, the more likely...

- it is that you will continue to fill your Body Image Vault with negative thoughts and feelings about your body and that these will multiply and take over your Vault

- it is that you will keep behaving in self-defeating ways, leaving your Vault's defence system in tatters

- you are to be negatively influenced by life experiences and interactions with others, as well as by other potential influences, which we will look at in the next chapter

- you are to get stuck in a vicious cycle of negative body image!

And that's exactly what the Body Image Thief wants. He wants:

- your Vault's defence system to remain in tatters

- you to think negative thoughts so that the positive, realistic and accepting ones you used to have in your Vault remain with him instead!

- you to get stuck in A VICIOUS CYCLE OF NEGATIVE BODY IMAGE!

We will look at each part of the vicious cycle of negative body image in more detail in the next few chapters. But before we do, have a go at drawing your own Body Image Vault and Body Image Thief in the Body Image Boxes provided.

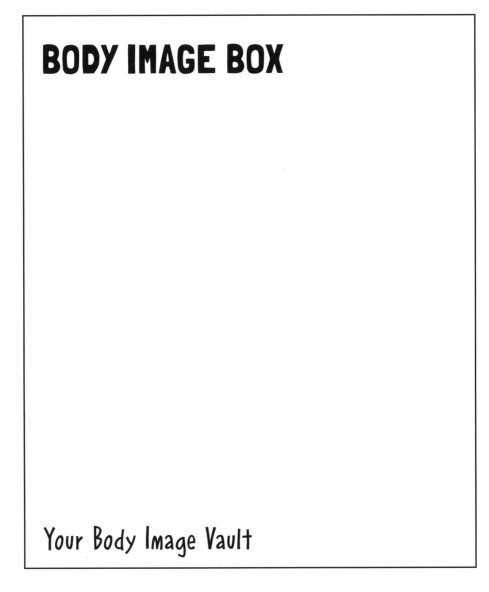

BODY IMAGE BOX

Your Body Image Vault

BODY IMAGE BOX

Your Body Image Thief

5

How a Negative Body Image Develops

Influences

As you saw in the previous chapter, how we think about our bodies and appearance-related situations can be influenced by a number of different factors. Although professionals still don't understand everything about influences on body image as yet, what they do know is that how we think about our bodies will be influenced by multiple factors and that the exact mix of factors will vary from person to person just like the ingredients of one baker's cake may vary from that of another baker!

EGGS   MILK   SUGAR   FLOUR

EGGS   SOYA MILK   HONEY   GLUTEN-FREE FLOUR

We are going to look at some of these potential influences for the rest of this chapter using stories from other young people, as this is Step 5 in improving your body image. Several of the factors that we will be looking at have the potential to be positive influences on us. However, for the purposes of this chapter, I will be focusing on their potential to be a negative influence on our body image by...

making us more likely to think and feel

in overly negative or unrealistic ways and fill our

Body Image Vaults with such thoughts and feelings.

But, just because each of the influences has the potential to do this, it doesn't mean that you have to think and feel in negative ways as a result. All these are merely POTENTIAL negative influences. You don't have to respond to them or your body in negative ways. You have a choice as to how you respond, which you will learn more about as we work through this book. And, as you will learn, it is making such choices that will banish your Body Image Thief.

The influences that we will be looking at can be divided into:

- *external influences* – come from outside of us
- *internal influences* – come from inside of us.

Let's start with the external ones.

Past and current life experiences

Every situation we go through in life has the potential to influence how we think and feel about our bodies. But difficult, stressful or traumatic experiences are more likely to have a negative influence. Such experiences can include:

- bullying
- neglect and abuse
- rejection
- humiliation
- accidents
- physical illnesses
- surgery
- relationship break-ups
- any other traumatic, stressful or difficult life experiences.

Let's see how one young person's body image was affected by their life experiences.

DWAYNE'S STORY

Eleven-year-old Dwayne recently started a new school and has been bullied every day by two boys in his class. They call Dwayne 'fatso', 'tubs' and other very cruel names. Dwayne cries when he looks in the mirror and blames himself for the bullying, telling himself that if he wasn't overweight he wouldn't be bullied. However, according to Dwayne's doctor, Dwayne isn't in fact overweight. But Dwayne can't get what the boys say out of his mind. Dwayne has started to make himself sick after eating.

In a 2006 national bullying survey by Bullying Online, over half of the bullying experienced by the young people surveyed was because of appearance.

Q. Have you ever experienced bullying or cyberbullying in relation to your appearance? Tick which answer applies to you.

    a) Yes   ☐   b) No   ☐

Q. If yes, how did it make you feel?

....
....
....

Q. And what effects did it have on you and your body image?

....
....
....

Now, in the next Body Image Box, write down experiences that you have been through that you believe have had a negative influence on your body image. Then write down how you thought and felt about your body in response to those experiences and any ways in which you acted as a result.

BODY IMAGE BOX

LIFE EXPERIENCE	MY THOUGHTS ABOUT MY BODY	MY FEELINGS TOWARDS MY BODY	HOW I ACTED AS A RESULT

Interactions with others

Q. Have you ever said or done anything that might have had a negative influence on how someone else felt about their body? If so, describe this below.

....

....

....

....

Our interactions with our family, friends, peers and other important people in our lives can also have an influence on our body image because:

- we can learn from the way our family members and friends respond to their own bodies and develop similar ways of responding ourselves

- we may judge our own bodies based on the comments that other people make about them and about the importance of appearance. These comments can be made through:

  - teasing and bullying

  - other people talking about how you look to your face or behind your back

  - unrealistic parental expectations about your appearance

  - talking with your friends and family about your body, weight and dieting, which is known as 'body talk'

  - family and peer pressure to change your looks in some way

  - family members comparing you to siblings who are physically different to you.

Let's see how one young person's body image was affected by their interactions with others.

JEZ'S STORY

Seventeen-year-old Jez broke his nose playing rugby. His mum now talks a lot about his nose and how she wishes he had his 'old nose back, as it made him look so handsome'. She also offered to buy Jez a 'nose job' for his 18th birthday. Jez has become very self-conscious about his nose and has started to avoid looking in the mirror. He believes that people are always looking at his nose and laughing about it behind his back.

In the Body Image Box below, write down any negative influences you think the following people have had on your body image.

BODY IMAGE BOX

Your friends:

....
....
....
....

Your parents:

....
....
....
....

Your siblings or other relatives:

....
....
....
....

Other young people you know:

....

....

....

....

Your teachers:

....

....

....

....

Pressure in sports

Taking part in sporting activities can be an incredibly rewarding and positive thing to do for many young people as it can bring a vast array of benefits in terms of health, wellbeing, sense of achievement, social interaction, future career options and much more.

However, for some people, taking part in sports can bring with it certain pressures that can influence the development of body image issues. These pressures can include:

- requirements to be a specific weight in order to take part in the sport

- focusing on appearance as well as performance within the sport

- unrealistic expectations from sporting coaches

- negative stereotypes that society can have about males and females in certain sports.

Let's see how one young person's body image was affected by pressure in sports.

VICTOR'S STORY

Victor is 13 years old and goes to his local gymnastics club. Some older boys at school make offensive comments to Victor, including calling him a 'wimp' for taking part in a 'girl's sport'. Victor is also under a lot of pressure to prepare for an important gymnastics competition that is coming up. As a result, he increased his muscle-building exercises six months ago. He wants to be in the best physical shape he can be in order to improve his performance at the competition, but he also wants to prove to the boys at school that he is a true 'man'. However, every time Victor looks in the mirror, he isn't happy with the results he sees. He can't get the word 'wimp' out of his head. He has now started to exercise to excess.

Societal messages about ideal body types

Society communicates messages to us on what the 'ideal' or 'perfect' body should look like. This 'ideal' has changed throughout history. For example, for females the following applied:

- In the middle ages and the Renaissance era, it was a full-figured body that was idealised as it symbolised wealth and fertility.

- In the 1920s, the ideal body type was slim, angular looking and flat-chested.

- In the 1950s, the curvy body shapes of Hollywood actresses such as Marilyn Monroe were idealised.

- In the 1960s, being thin like the model Twiggy was the ideal.

- In the 1990s, the tall, slender figures of the 'supermodels' were the ideal.

Today, within Western societies, the following ideals are portrayed for females:

- *The thin figure*, i.e. the US 'size zero' (which equates to size 4 in the UK and size 32–34 in Europe and is the same waist size as the average 8-year-old girl!), but also with moderate-to-large breasts.

- *The curvy, toned figure*, i.e. fit and toned, but with 'hourglass curves' at the breasts, hips and buttocks.

For males, the messages about what constitutes an 'ideal' masculine body have changed throughout history too and in the following ways:

- In the nineteenth century, it was a plump figure that was idealised as it symbolised wealth.
- In the 1920s, a thin and fit figure was idealised as it became associated with wealth and with action and Western films.
- From the 1950s onwards, physical fitness became the focus of the 'ideal' male physique as bodybuilding and the fitness industry grew in popularity.

In today's Western society, the main physique that has become idealised for men involves:

- an average build
- a slender waist and hips
- muscular arms, shoulders, chest and stomach
- low body fat.

These messages about the 'ideal' body types appear to jump out at us everywhere we look and from so many sectors of society, including:

- the media (such as newspapers, magazines, TV programmes, films, music videos, computer games, the internet and social networking sites)
- the advertising industry
- the beauty and fashion industries
- the fitness and diet industries
- the cosmetic surgery industry
- children's products
- government health campaigns.

THE MEDIA AND ADVERTISING INDUSTRIES

Within the media and advertising industries the following have become commonplace:

- Images of models and celebrities are chosen to reflect today's body 'ideals'.

- Other body types are ignored.

- Digitally altered images are used so that they meet the body 'ideals' (which we will look at in more detail later on in this workbook).

- People with 'ideal' body images are shown as leading successful and happy lives.

- People who don't live up to the body ideals are stereotyped in negative ways, used as the butt of jokes or used to advertise weight-loss products.

- Adult actors and actresses with adult 'ideal' bodies are chosen to play teenage characters in TV programmes and films.

- TV schedules are filled with 'make-over' programmes and magazines contain numerous articles on how to improve your looks.

And with the increase in social media, people are also now:

- judging themselves based upon comments from strangers on social networking sites

- digitally enhancing their own photographs before they load them onto such sites

- asking others to comment on whether they are attractive by uploading videos of themselves online.

BEAUTY, FASHION, FITNESS, DIET AND COSMETIC SURGERY INDUSTRIES

Within these industries the following is taking place:

- Digitally altered images are often being used to sell products and services.

- Body types that differ from the 'ideals' are rarely used in advertisements or on the fashion catwalks.

- New products and services aimed at helping us to 'improve' or 'fix' our appearance are being produced all the time.

But some beauty and fashion companies are now recognising that they need to do more to promote a variety of body types and images of masculinity and femininity. This includes:

- Debenhams using more diverse models for fashion campaigns and plus-sized mannequins in their stores

- Boots advertising beauty products with images that haven't been airbrushed

- Dove sponsoring extensive research into self-esteem and body image in females and placing a variety of information and resources on their website to help young women be confident in who they are, just as they are.

CHILDREN'S PRODUCTS

Children's products also send out messages about appearance. For example, consider the following:

- If Barbie was a real woman she would be unable to hold the weight of her breasts due to her slender frame and she would be severely underweight.

- Children's action figures now have bulging muscles and dolls have heavy make-up.

- 'Baddies' are often portrayed as unattractive and the heroes and heroines as attractive in children's fairy stories, cartoons and films.

Thus, we are being bombarded every day with messages about how we 'should' look and about the importance of appearance. As a result, it is hard not to take these messages on board. It is hard not to compare yourself to the 'ideal' images, as the following edition of *The Body Image Times* shows.

THE BODY IMAGE TIMES
SOCIETAL INFLUENCES
ON BODY IMAGE

A 2012 survey by Girl Guiding UK of both males and females found that 59 per cent of the young people surveyed felt pressure to look the way that celebrities do, with this rising to 72 per cent for 16–21-year-olds.

A 2007 study by Harrison and Bond found that looking at computer gaming magazines makes boys want to become more muscular.

And in a study by Credos in 2011 of females aged 10–21 years, the following was found:

- Thirty-seven per cent of the young women surveyed wanted to look like the models they see in adverts.

- Forty-seven per cent agreed with the statement 'Seeing adverts using thin models makes me want to diet/lose weight/feel more conscious of the way I look'.

The Body Image Times, Page 1

Here's how one young person's body image was affected by societal messages.

MEGAN'S STORY

Fourteen-year-old Megan has been reading fashion, beauty and celebrity gossip magazines since she was 10 years old. She cuts pictures out of the magazines and sticks them on her bedroom wall to remind herself of what a 'perfect' girl should look like. She compares how she looks in the mirror to these pictures every night. She hates what she sees in the mirror and has started to skip meals in an effort to become as thin as the females in her magazines.

GOVERNMENT HEALTH CAMPAIGNS

Societal messages that are communicated for our benefit can also sometimes have an unexpected negative impact. Anti-obesity campaigns are one example of this. They teach us about the importance of balanced eating and fitness for our health, which is obviously a good thing. However, phrases such as 'the war against obesity' and 'obesity epidemic' are being heard more and more in response to these campaigns and some children and young people are starting to believe that gaining weight is a thing to dread and fear. Combine this with the fact that children and young people are being teased, isolated, bullied and stereotyped due to their weight by others and again you can see how societal messages can influence our body image, even when they are given for our benefit.

Having read all of the above, think for a minute about your own views on the 'ideal' body and answer the questions in the Body Image Box below.

BODY IMAGE BOX

How would you describe the 'ideal' male body?

....

....

....

....

How would you describe the 'ideal' female body?

....

....

....

....

What kinds of words do you and your friends use when talking about 'ideal' body types?

....

....

....

....

What things have influenced your view of the 'ideal' body types?

....

....

....

....

Who do you think has the 'ideal' male body type?

....

....

....

....

Who do you think has the 'ideal' female body type?

....

....

....

....

Now let's look at the internal factors that can have a potential influence on how we think and feel about our bodies.

Other emotional or mental health issues

If you have experienced another type of emotional or mental health issue in the past or are suffering from one in the here and now, such as anxiety, depression, stress or an eating disorder, it may make you more likely to develop body image issues. Also, if you experience low self-esteem or low self-confidence in relation to other aspects of yourself, you may be more susceptible to the development of a negative body image. Let's see how one young person's body image was affected by experiencing other emotional issues.

CARA'S STORY

Twelve-year-old Cara has been lacking in confidence for several years. She always doubts her abilities even though she is highly intelligent and an excellent musician. Cara has a number of friends but doesn't understand why anyone would like her. She also criticises herself and puts herself down regularly. Recently Cara's self-doubts and self-criticisms have spread to how she looks. She has started to use words like 'ugly' and 'disgusting' when she talks about herself. She also pulled out of a school musical recital last week because of a worry that everyone would be thinking how 'ugly' she was while she played the piano.

Mental health issues can sometimes run in families. So if you have a family history of body image-related mental health issues, such as body dysmorphic disorder or eating disorders, you may have an increased risk of developing a mental health issue yourself, including a body image-related mental health issue. Here's how one young person's body image was affected by mental health issues in his family.

AARON'S STORY

Aaron is 13 years old. His uncle was diagnosed with body dysmorphic disorder when he was 19 years old. Over the past year, Aaron has become more and more preoccupied with his eyes. They are not completely symmetrical and Aaron believes that this makes him ugly. He thinks it is highly noticeable to other people and believes it to be the reason why his girlfriend recently dumped him two months ago even though she told him that it wasn't.

But even if you have suffered or are suffering with some form of emotional or mental health issue, it doesn't have to mean that you will also develop a body image issue. Also, even though one of your grandparents, parents or siblings had or has a mental health issue, it doesn't mean that you have to develop one too. But even if you do develop a body image-related mental health issue, you can learn to manage it.

Personality traits

Certain personality traits, such as perfectionism, shyness or obsessiveness, can sometimes make us more likely to develop body image issues. Here's how one young person's body image was affected by one of their personality traits.

DEBBIE'S STORY

Sixteen-year-old Debbie is a perfectionist. She gets annoyed with herself if she doesn't get full marks in school exams and if she doesn't play 'perfectly' in her school netball team matches. She also believes that she needs to look 'perfect', otherwise her friends will stop liking her. She spends several hours getting ready for school every morning and even longer getting ready for parties. But she is never happy with how she looks and cries herself to sleep most nights. She believes that she needs to work harder in order to achieve perfection. As a result, the time she spends getting ready for school every morning is increasing and she has started to arrive at school late.

However, it is important to remember that even though you may have a personality trait that makes you more susceptible to developing a body image issue, it doesn't mean that you will develop one.

Actual appearance and physical alterations to our appearance

Our actual appearance, especially if there is an aspect of it that makes us stand out from others, has the potential to have an influence on our body image. Alterations to our appearance can also have an impact upon our body image, including those alterations that occur as a result of:

- illness
- developing an injury, disfigurement or disability
- side effects from medical treatments
- surgery

- puberty

- pregnancy.

Here's how one young person's body image was affected by an alteration to her appearance.

DEENA'S STORY

Fifteen-year-old Deena was injured in an accident and had to have one of her legs amputated below the knee. Deena has made massive progress in her physical recovery and uses a prosthetic leg. However, she feels different from everyone else around her due to the amputation. She wears long trousers all the time to hide her prosthetic leg, but still worries that strangers will notice it. Since returning to school, she has become preoccupied with thoughts that everyone in her class is staring at her leg. She refuses to take part in physical education classes because she is afraid of what people will say if they were to see her prosthetic leg. She is worried that she will never get a boyfriend because she believes her amputation makes her disfigured, abnormal and unattractive.

In the next Body Image Box, list any internal factors that you believe have had a negative influence on your body image.

BODY IMAGE BOX

Negative internal influences on my body image

Throughout this chapter, you have learnt about a variety of different factors that have the potential to influence how we think and feel about our bodies, and you have identified which of these factors have had an influence on you.

But remember that although these factors have had a negative influence on your body image in the past, they don't have to continue to do so in the future. They DO NOT CAUSE you to develop a negative body image; they just make you MORE SUSCEPTIBLE to:

- thinking and feeling in a negative way about your body

- acting in self-defeating ways

- leaving your Body Image Vault vulnerable to your Body Image Thief!

But you have a choice to think and act differently, as you will learn later in this workbook, in order to banish your Body Image Thief for good!

How a Negative Body Image Develops

Thoughts

Understanding more about your body image-related thoughts is Step 6 in improving your body image. So let's take a look at the kinds of thoughts that can end up in our Body Image Vaults.

Types of thoughts

Our thoughts are made up of two types:

OUR DEEPER BELIEFS	OUR EVERYDAY THOUGHTS
These are general assumptions or rules that we have about ourselves, other people, the world around us and our future.	These are the thoughts we have every single day in response to the specific situations that we go through.

We can fill our Body Image Vaults with both deeper beliefs and everyday thoughts. Let's look at each in more detail.

Deeper beliefs

Our deeper beliefs can be:

realistic and positive

or

unrealistic and overly negative.

The internal and external influences that we looked at in the previous chapter have the potential to influence which kinds of deeper beliefs we develop. And over time, these beliefs become fixed in our minds as we tend to focus on evidence that we think supports our deeper beliefs and dismiss or ignore any evidence that goes against them. Thus, our deeper beliefs become strict and inflexible rules that we live by and assumptions that we believe in 100 per cent. We very rarely challenge their accuracy, taking it for granted that they are true.

And as a result, we interpret every situation we go through in life based upon these beliefs. Thus, the way we think every day about everything we experience and the way we think about ourselves in response to those experiences is guided by these deeper beliefs.

Let's take a look at this further by imagining you have a compass that guides you through life.

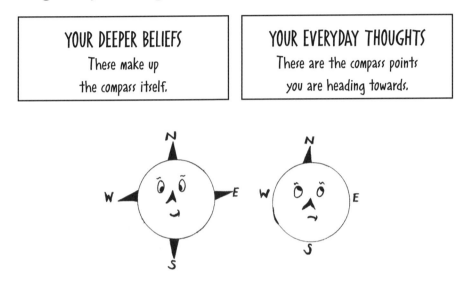

YOUR DEEPER BELIEFS	YOUR EVERYDAY THOUGHTS
These make up the compass itself.	These are the compass points you are heading towards.

FULLY WORKING COMPASS = FIXED POSITIVE AND REALISTIC DEEPER BELIEFS

When you have a compass that is working correctly, it will guide you to the points that you need to get to in order to make the progress you want to make. The same applies to your deeper beliefs. When your deeper beliefs are realistic they will guide you to think in realistic ways on a day-to-day basis about events, people and yourself, thus helping you to progress through life in a positive way. And your Body Image Vault becomes full of these realistic deeper beliefs and everyday thoughts.

BROKEN-DOWN COMPASS = FIXED UNREALISTIC AND OVERLY NEGATIVE DEEPER BELIEFS

However, if your compass starts to break down, its needle might start to occasionally stick at a particular direction, such as north, making it more likely for you to go north on occasions even if you want to go east, west or south. The same also applies to your deeper beliefs. If you start to develop deeper beliefs that are unrealistic or overly negative in some way, you can start to become more likely to think everyday thoughts that are also unrealistic and overly negative. Thus these start to accumulate in your Body Image Vault.

If your compass's needle eventually gets totally stuck on north over time, you will then always be guided north by it, even if you want to go east, west or south. And once again, the same applies to your deeper beliefs. If the unrealistic and overly negative deeper beliefs get stronger and stronger in your mind over time, until eventually you believe in them 100 per cent and take it for granted that they are true, then it becomes very likely that you will normally be guided towards unrealistic and overly negative thoughts about events, people and yourself on a day-to-day basis.

It is this combination of unrealistic and overly negative deeper beliefs and everyday thoughts that you fill your Body Image Vault with when you are developing a negative body image. And as you get stuck in a cycle of unrealistic and overly negative ways of thinking and believing, your Vault gets fuller and fuller with these types of thoughts and beliefs, especially as these are the ones that the Body Image Thief leaves behind!

Types of negative body image-related deeper beliefs

The unrealistic and overly negative deeper beliefs that people with a negative body image commonly have in their Body Image Vault include the following:

- If I'm not 'perfect' looking, I'm ugly.
- If I'm not 'perfect' looking, I'm a worthless person.
- I need to look 'perfect' in order to be happy.
- If I look better, my life will be better.
- If I don't look 'perfect', my life will be ruined.
- I need to look 'perfect' to be liked and accepted.
- If I have flaws in my appearance, people will notice.
- If I don't look 'perfect', people won't like me.
- If I don't look 'perfect', I'm not trying hard enough.

These deeper beliefs are based on assumptions that:

- your appearance alone determines how worthy you are as a person
- you have to conform to society's idea of what makes a 'perfect' body in order to live a successful life and be liked and loved by others
- your appearance is to blame for negative things that have happened
- controlling your appearance in some way is the only way to make you feel better
- only a 'perfect' appearance leads to happiness.

In the Body Image Box on the next page, have a go at writing down any deeper beliefs that you have that relate to your body image in some way. If you struggle to do this at this stage, don't worry, as we will return to this when we look at how we can manage our thoughts in order to improve our body image later in the workbook.

BODY IMAGE BOX

My deeper beliefs

Types of negative body image-related everyday thoughts

Psychologists have a name for patterns of everyday thoughts that are unrealistic and overly negative. They call them...

thinking errors.

The following are common types of thinking errors experienced by people with a negative body image:

- *All or nothing thinking* – Thinking in absolute terms or black and white terms with no shades of grey. It's thinking in extremes. For example, Mandy, aged 10, thinks 'I am horrendously ugly'.

- *Overgeneralising* – Thinking that what happens in a one-off event is a sign of a long-lasting pattern. For example, Tom, aged 13, thinks 'The fact that a girl at school made fun of my hair means no-one will ever think I'm good looking'.

- *Fortune telling* – Making predictions that things will turn out badly in the future. For example, Toni, aged 11, thinks 'If I go to my friend's party, I will get laughed at because of the wart on my face'.

- *Catastrophising* – Jumping to the worst-case scenario. For example, Brendan, aged 15, thinks 'I will always be alone and unhappy'.

- *Mind reading* – Making negative assumptions about what other people are thinking about you without actually knowing what they are thinking. For example, Poppy, aged 14, thinks 'All my friends think I look like a freak'.

- *Magnification* – Blowing your flaws out of proportion. For example, Neil, aged 12, thinks 'My birthmark on my cheek is the only thing people see when they look at me – it's so ugly'.

- *Negative comparisons* – Comparing yourself negatively to others. For example, Sharon, aged 14, thinks 'All the girls in my class are prettier than me', and Phil, aged 16, thinks 'I'll never look like the guys in the magazines'.

- *Unrealistic expectations* – Thinking about yourself in terms of 'I should' or 'I must' or 'I have to'. For example, Bella, aged 15, thinks 'I have to look perfect for the party tonight'.

- *Focusing on the negatives* – Such as in situations, in other people's comments or in how you look. For example, Denise, aged 13, thinks 'All that matters is my spotty skin. My nice hair and eyes don't count'.

- *Disbelieving the positives* – Treating positive information as false or twisting it into negatives. For example, Mohammad, aged 16, thinks 'The girl I like at school only said she liked my new haircut because she felt sorry for me'.

- *Putting yourself down* – Thinking in very critical ways about yourself. For example, Craig, aged 11, thinks 'I'm an unattractive wimp'.

- *Blaming your appearance* – Thinking that everything that goes wrong is because of your appearance. For example, Winona, aged 15, thinks 'My appearance has ruined my life'.

- *Emotional reasoning* – Thinking that because something feels true to you, it is true. For example, Patrick, aged 10, thinks 'I feel disgusted when I look in the mirror, so I must be disgusting'.

- *'I can't' thinking* – Doubting your ability to do something because of your appearance. For example, Serena, aged 14, thinks 'I can't go to the beach until I lose some weight'.

It's also important to note that because we all like or dislike different parts of our bodies our thinking errors will be based upon different parts of our bodies. For example, one person's thinking errors might relate to how their nose looks, while another person's might relate to the muscle tone in their arms. Another person's thinking errors might relate to a disability or disfigurement that they have had from birth or that they have developed as a result of a trauma. Another person's thinking errors might relate to a slight scar that is hardly noticeable, whereas another person's might relate to an appearance flaw that they believe is there even though it doesn't exist.

Also, some people's thinking errors will relate to one body part, whereas other people's can involve several body parts or their body as a whole. Some people will remain preoccupied with thoughts about the same body part for many years, while another person may add to their body concerns over the years or stop being concerned by the original body part and start being concerned by another.

Let's now take a look at your thinking errors. In the Body Image Box below, colour in or highlight which of the following thinking errors tend to apply to your patterns of everyday thoughts about your body.

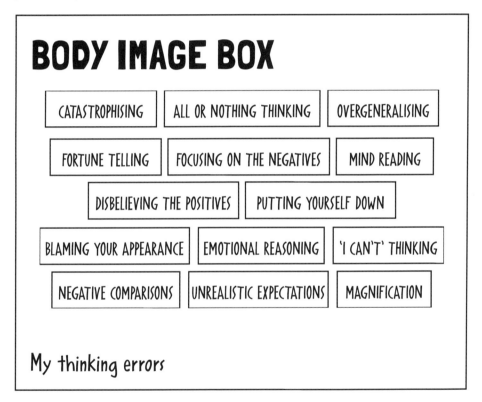

BODY IMAGE BOX

| CATASTROPHISING | ALL OR NOTHING THINKING | OVERGENERALISING |

| FORTUNE TELLING | FOCUSING ON THE NEGATIVES | MIND READING |

| DISBELIEVING THE POSITIVES | PUTTING YOURSELF DOWN |

| BLAMING YOUR APPEARANCE | EMOTIONAL REASONING | 'I CAN'T' THINKING |

| NEGATIVE COMPARISONS | UNREALISTIC EXPECTATIONS | MAGNIFICATION |

My thinking errors

It is normal for all of us to have thinking errors about our bodies every so often. However, when you are stuck in the vicious cycle of negative body image, these thinking errors become more and more frequent. After a while, these thinking errors can start to go round and round and round in your mind until it feels like you can't get them out of there and they clog up your Body Image Vault. And they can reinforce your overly negative or unrealistic deeper beliefs about appearance and lead you to feel a variety of negative emotions. These also pile up in your Body Image Vault.

We will have a look at these feelings in the next chapter as understanding body image-related feelings is Step 7 in improving your body image.

7

How a Negative Body Image Develops

Feelings

If you tend to think in unrealistic and overly negative ways about your body and in response to appearance-related situations, then you are likely to experience negative feelings about your body too. Listed in the boxes below are some of the common negative feelings that people with a negative body image have in their Body Image Vaults.

UNHAPPINESS
DISSATISFACTION
FEELING UNCOMFORTABLE IN OWN BODY
DISTRESS
UPSET
SHAME
A SENSE OF FAILURE
ANXIETY
PANIC
SELF-CONSCIOUSNESS
LOW MOOD
SELF-BLAME
GUILT
FEAR
TENSION
EMBARRASSMENT
SADNESS
ANGER

F E E L I N G S

FRUSTRATION
ENVY
HUMILIATION
DISGUST
SELF-LOATHING
HOPELESSNESS
INSECURITY
CONFUSION
FEELING ISOLATED
FEELING REJECTED
DISAPPOINTMENT
HELPLESSNESS
JEALOUSY
SENSE OF INADEQUACY
SENSE OF INFERIORITY
PARANOIA
LONELINESS
WORTHLESSNESS
STRESS

If you think and feel in unrealistic and overly negative ways about your body, it is very likely that you will then start to act in self-defeating ways in response to these thoughts and feelings. This then leaves your Body Image Vault vulnerable to your Body Image Thief! We will look at these types of behaviours in the next chapter, as understanding your body image-related behaviours is Step 8 in improving your body image.

How a Negative Body Image Develops

Behaviours

A person with unrealistic and overly negative deeper beliefs who is having everyday thinking errors and feeling negatively about their body is likely to behave in at least one of the following ways:

AVOIDANCE	HIDING	CHECKING	FIXING

We may AVOID situations or HIDE parts of our bodies, as we think it is the only way of preventing other people from seeing how bad we look, and stopping bad things happening and us experiencing distress as a result. For example, Pippa avoids mirrors because of her appearance concerns and Matty hides his physique under baggy clothes.

We may also CHECK or try to FIX aspects of our bodies over and over again not because we want to but because we think we have to in order to feel better about our bodies and because we believe bad things will happen and we will experience distress if we don't. For example, Wendy checks her appearance regularly in the mirror. Plus, Natasha spends a fortune on beauty products, Anthony has pectoral implants, Kevin uses steroids and Chrissie swaps from one diet to the next, all in an effort to fix their appearance.

These are what we call...

self-defeating behaviours.

This is because they have a negative impact on us in the long term and leave our Body Image Vaults vulnerable to the Body Image Thief!

Let's look at each of these types of self-defeating behaviours in more detail.

Avoidance

As you have just read, people with a negative body image have a tendency to avoid certain situations that provoke distress over how they look. Examples of the kinds of situations that are commonly avoided include the following:

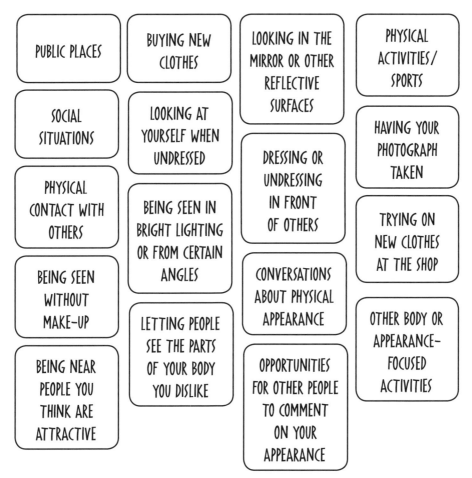

As we have seen, avoidance is understandable when you have body image concerns as it is a short-term way of keeping your body image-related distress low. However, in the long term, avoidance does not help and it causes our Body Image Vault's defence system to break down, leaving it vulnerable to the Body Image Thief! The following story highlights why.

GARY'S STORY

Gary is 10 years old. It is time for him to start school swimming lessons. Gary wants to learn to swim as he wants to join the Navy when he gets older. However, he avoids going for the first three weeks by pretending to be ill on those days. Gary believes he will look fat and ugly in his swimming shorts, that everyone in his class will laugh at him and that his school life will be awful from that point forward. So avoiding the lessons is the only thing Gary can think to do.

Q. What are the advantages of avoidance for Gary?

....
....
....

Q. What are the disadvantages of avoidance for Gary?

....
....
....

You may have written that the advantage for Gary is he avoids experiencing any distress. However, the disadvantages include:

- not giving himself the chance to see that the bad things he is predicting will happen are actually unlikely to happen

- not giving himself the chance to see that even if the bad thing happened he would be able to cope

- missing out on doing something that he really wants to be able to do

- making it harder for him to fulfil his ambitions for the future.

I'd like you to list anything that you avoid on a regular basis because of body image concerns in the next Body Image Box. And then I want you to write down what you think the advantages and disadvantages of each are.

BODY IMAGE BOX

SITUATIONS I AM AVOIDING	ADVANTAGES OF AVOIDING	DISADVANTAGES OF AVOIDING

Hiding

Hiding is another behaviour that some people use in order to prevent other people seeing how they really look and bad things happening as a result. Let's see how one young person hides a part of her body from others.

TERRI'S STORY

Terri, aged 13, hates the fact that she has a lazy left eye. She believes that it is really noticeable to others and makes her unattractive. She wears sunglasses as much as possible and the rest of the time she tries to hide her eye with her hair or her hand.

Common types of hiding behaviours include:

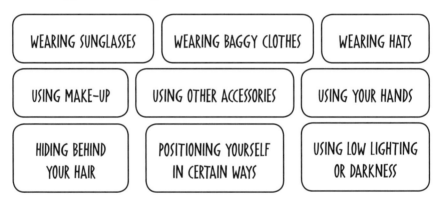

WEARING SUNGLASSES   WEARING BAGGY CLOTHES   WEARING HATS

USING MAKE-UP   USING OTHER ACCESSORIES   USING YOUR HANDS

HIDING BEHIND YOUR HAIR   POSITIONING YOURSELF IN CERTAIN WAYS   USING LOW LIGHTING OR DARKNESS

But although hiding may bring short-term benefits, it also brings long-term disadvantages, including leaving your Body Image Vault vulnerable to the Body Image Thief.

I'd like you to list the ways that you try to hide your body or a part of your body on a regular basis in the next Body Image Box. And then I want you to write down what you think the advantages and disadvantages of each are.

BODY IMAGE BOX

MY HIDING BEHAVIOURS	ADVANTAGES OF MY HIDING BEHAVIOURS	DISADVANTAGES OF MY HIDING BEHAVIOURS

Checking

Some people believe they have to check their bodies in order to feel better about their appearance and to prevent bad things from happening as a result of their appearance. Let's see how one young person checks his body.

DEAN'S STORY

Dean, aged 16, hates the size of his muscles in his arms. He doesn't believe they are as muscular as they need to be and pokes, prods and flexes them numerous times each day. He also constantly asks others what they think about his arm muscles.

Common forms of checking behaviours include:

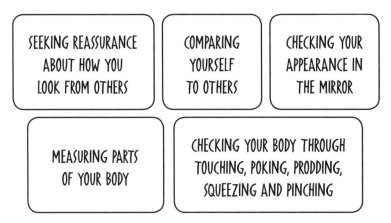

SEEKING REASSURANCE ABOUT HOW YOU LOOK FROM OTHERS

COMPARING YOURSELF TO OTHERS

CHECKING YOUR APPEARANCE IN THE MIRROR

MEASURING PARTS OF YOUR BODY

CHECKING YOUR BODY THROUGH TOUCHING, POKING, PRODDING, SQUEEZING AND PINCHING

However, these behaviours only lead to negative impacts in the long term and leave our Body Image Vaults vulnerable to the Body Image Thief!

In the next Body Image Box, list the different ways that you check your body or parts of your body on a regular basis and what you think the advantages and disadvantages of doing these are.

BODY IMAGE BOX

MY CHECKING BEHAVIOURS	ADVANTAGES OF MY CHECKING BEHAVIOURS	DISADVANTAGES OF MY CHECKING BEHAVIOURS

Fixing

Fixing involves trying to adjust or alter or improve your appearance in some way. People with a negative body image often believe they have to fix their appearance in order to feel better and to prevent bad things from happening. Common forms of fixing behaviours include:

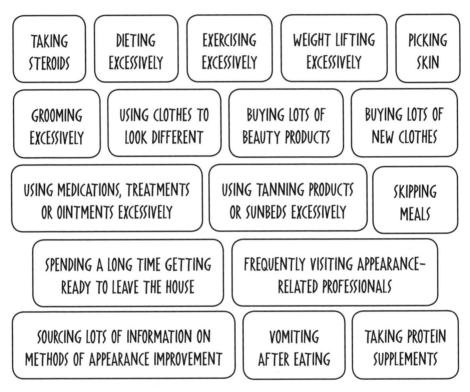

TAKING STEROIDS	DIETING EXCESSIVELY

TAKING STEROIDS   DIETING EXCESSIVELY   EXERCISING EXCESSIVELY   WEIGHT LIFTING EXCESSIVELY   PICKING SKIN

GROOMING EXCESSIVELY   USING CLOTHES TO LOOK DIFFERENT   BUYING LOTS OF BEAUTY PRODUCTS   BUYING LOTS OF NEW CLOTHES

USING MEDICATIONS, TREATMENTS OR OINTMENTS EXCESSIVELY   USING TANNING PRODUCTS OR SUNBEDS EXCESSIVELY   SKIPPING MEALS

SPENDING A LONG TIME GETTING READY TO LEAVE THE HOUSE   FREQUENTLY VISITING APPEARANCE-RELATED PROFESSIONALS

SOURCING LOTS OF INFORMATION ON METHODS OF APPEARANCE IMPROVEMENT   VOMITING AFTER EATING   TAKING PROTEIN SUPPLEMENTS

Let's see how one young person tries to fix how she looks.

MARTHA'S STORY

Martha, aged 17, hates her complexion. She spends all the money she earns from her part-time job on trips to beauty therapists and has had her parents pay for numerous visits to a dermatologist. She uses various creams and ointments on her face several times a day and she picks at the spots on her face for at least an hour every day.

However, these behaviours lead to negative impacts in the long term and leave our Body Image Vaults vulnerable to the Body Image Thief!

In the Body Image Box below, list the different ways in which you often try to 'fix' your appearance and the advantages and disadvantages of each.

BODY IMAGE BOX

MY FIXING BEHAVIOURS	ADVANTAGES OF MY FIXING BEHAVIOURS	DISADVANTAGES OF MY FIXING BEHAVIOURS

Avoiding, hiding, checking and fixing behaviours may help us to feel better in the short term. However, in the long term, they just keep us trapped in the vicious cycle of negative body image because they:

- keep us focused on the perceived flaws in our appearance
- lead us to think that we have to keep doing them
- prevent us from seeing that the bad things we worry about happening are unlikely to happen whether we avoided, hid, checked or fixed in these ways or not
- reduce our confidence in our ability to handle similar situations next time without avoiding, hiding, checking or fixing
- prevent us from finding out that even if our predictions did happen they might not be as bad as we think and that we would cope
- prevent us from finding out what would have happened if we hadn't avoided, hidden, checked or fixed
- prevent us from finding out that the assumptions we make aren't realistic or accurate
- reinforce our unrealistic and overly negative thoughts as well as our negative feelings about our bodies
- reinforce our inaccurate view that our appearance is to blame for what we are feeling
- waste a lot of our time that we could be spending on more fun, enjoyable and healthier experiences instead
- lead us to do things that are dangerous for us health wise, such as under-eating, excessive exercising, taking steroids, binging and purging, excessive use of laxatives or weight-loss aids, etc.
- take away the enjoyment of grooming activities that are supposed to be seen as fun, not as compulsory!
- hinder us from living life to the full
- hinder us from achieving what we want to
- affect our relationships with others

- prevent us from discovering more constructive and positive ways to cope with our body image concerns

- cause our Body Image Vault's defence system to break down, allowing the Body Image Thief to steal from our Vault!

Now let's take a look at the impacts that having a negative body image can have on us and our lives.

9

Impacts of a Negative Body Image

Understanding the impacts of having a negative body image is Step 9 in improving your body image. Write down in the Body Image Box below how you think your body image has affected you and your life.

BODY IMAGE BOX

Impacts of my negative body image on me and my life

Here are some stories from other young people about how their negative body image has impacted on them.

'As my body image has got more and more negative, I have found it harder and harder to cope with the feelings that I have. I started self-harming about a year ago and I now have to hide my body even more than I did before.' (Jessica, 13)

'I feel like I have to avoid so many situations because of my worries about my looks. I am so afraid of people rejecting me or laughing at me because of how I look that I just can't face being around people. I stopped going to football practice and karate classes which I used to love. I hate having to go to school every day. I can't concentrate because I can't stop thinking about how I must look to other people. It's got so bad that my grades have really slipped.' (Lewis, 15)

'I feel like I have to spend so long looking in the mirror and grooming that I never end up actually leaving the house to go out with my friends. Most of them have given up on me at this stage as they got fed up of me letting them down. I always feared that I'd end up alone if I didn't look good enough. It turns out that by trying to look good enough I've ended up alone.' (Chloe, 14)

'I convinced myself that I needed to lose weight in order to fit in at my new school. All the girls were so thin and so pretty and I just felt like a fat blimp next to them. The problem was that the diets just weren't working. In the end I started to make myself sick after eating. I have been doing this every day for over a year. But I don't feel any better for it. My skin looks awful, the dentist tells me I've destroyed the enamel on my teeth and I'm just tired all the time. I live in fear every day that people at school will find out what I'm doing as I make myself sick in the school toilets too after lunch. I hate my body. I hate me.' (Issy, 16)

'I started to become obsessed with working out a couple of years ago. Other boys in my class at school were developing quicker than I was and I felt like such a weakling compared to them. I was always the girls' funny friend but never their boyfriend. So I started working out a few times a week. But the more workouts I did, the more I wanted to do. I just wasn't becoming as muscular as I wanted to be. It wasn't long before I was using my pocket money to buy protein shakes. But they just weren't enough. I started using steroids and now the girls don't think of me as their funny friend, they think of me as the guy to avoid. My moods are so up and down. I get so angry and irritable at times. I know I wanted to be a different version of me, but not this version!' (Neil, 17)

'I spend so much time asking my mum if I look OK, if my make-up's OK, if my clothes are OK, if my hair is OK. I'm driving her mad and it's causing so many arguments between us. She tells me that I look beautiful and I have no need to worry, but that just makes me angry because I know she's only saying it to make me feel better. My mum and I used to get along so well and now we can barely say two words to each other without there being an argument. I miss how we used to be.' (Holly, 12)

'I hate what I see when I look in the mirror. All I see is my acne. I feel horrible and disgusting and I know everyone is thinking the same when they look at me. I pick at my skin for hours every day. But it only makes things worse. I have scars on my face from years of skin picking. I now hate what I see in the mirror even more.' (Jason, 16)

'I was a really good dancer and loved it. But then I started puberty before the other girls in my dance class. I hate how my body looks now. I feel like such a freak. I've stopped going dancing as I can't face people looking at me in my dance costumes. I wear baggy clothes all the time now to cover up my body. I just feel so down and different.' (Olivia, 11)

'All the other boys in my class pick on me because I wear glasses and have ginger hair. I'm sad all the time now and I'm angry that I was born this way. I feel so angry that I hit my bedroom wall a lot. I hurt my hand very badly last week.' (Greg, 10)

'When I look in the mirror all I see is a fat, ugly, worthless blob. So I exercise and exercise and exercise some more. I injured myself, but I continued to exercise. I've now seriously injured myself. I can't compete in the athletic tournaments for the season because of the injury. I don't know how I'm going to cope without being able to exercise. And what if I've messed up my dreams of being a top athlete?' (Tim, 15)

Now you've thought about the impacts that your negative body image has had on you and your life and you've read stories from other young people about the impacts a negative body image has had on them and their lives, try the activity below so as to help you summarise what all this has shown you.

Each of the six boxes that follows relates to an area of a person's life that can be impacted upon by having a negative body image. Write down in each box the ways you think having a negative body image can impact upon that aspect of a person's life.

PHYSICAL HEALTH

....
....
....
....
....
....
....

MENTAL HEALTH AND EMOTIONAL WELLBEING

....
....
....
....
....
....
....

RELATIONSHIPS

....
....
....
....
....
....
....

SOCIAL AND LEISURE ACTIVITIES

....
....
....
....
....
....
....

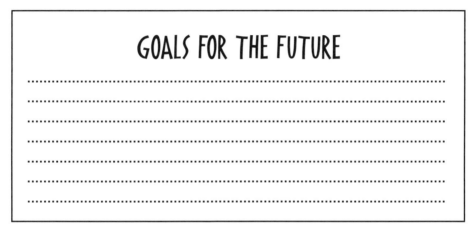

STUDIES AND WORK

....
....
....
....
....
....
....

GOALS FOR THE FUTURE

....
....
....
....
....
....
....

In the *Physical Health* box, you may have talked about the physical health impacts of behaviours such as:

- *skin picking*, which includes scarring and infections

- *excessive exercising*, which includes injury and exhaustion

- *eating too little*, which includes dangerous weight loss, exhaustion, lacking in vital vitamins and minerals, susceptibility to illnesses, acne, hair thinning or loss, as well as a range of serious health issues in the long term

- *binge eating and purging*, which includes damage to tooth enamel, damage to your oesophagus (the part of your body that takes your food from your throat to your stomach), and serious health issues in the long term

- *overeating*, which includes weight gain, acne, stomach and digestion problems, high cholesterol, high blood pressure and diabetes

- *steroid use*, which includes mood changes, liver and kidney damage, hair loss, acne, stomach problems, sleep disturbance and high blood pressure

- *unhealthy/yo-yo dieting*, which includes similar physical effects to the eating too little category discussed above, along with the likelihood of more rapid weight gain when you stop dieting.

Have a go at researching the dangers of one of the behaviours from the previous list and write them down in the Body Image Box that follows.

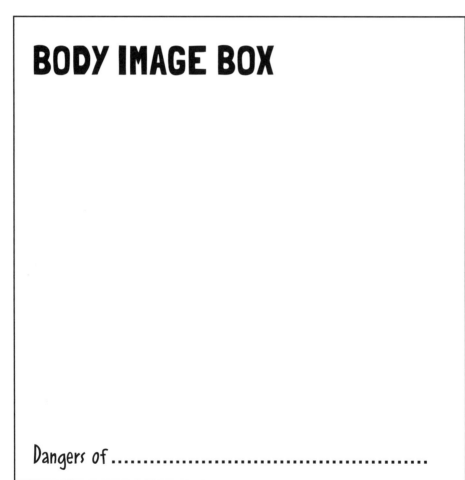

BODY IMAGE BOX

Dangers of ....

In the *Mental Health and Emotional Wellbeing* box, you may have listed some of the following emotional impacts of a negative body image (please note that there are many more):

- anxiety
- depression
- anger
- guilt
- self-loathing
- envy.

You may have also talked about the links between a negative body image and the development of other mental health conditions such as those listed below.

- *Anorexia nervosa* – This involves a fear of weight gain, believing oneself to be overweight even when severely underweight, and the pursuit of thinness through a variety of weight-loss methods, including excessive exercise, unhealthy and extreme dieting, self-induced vomiting and the use of weight-loss pills, enemas or laxatives.

- *Bulimia nervosa* – This involves frequent episodes of eating unusually large amounts of food (binges), often in secret, followed by purging (such as self-induced vomiting or the use of laxatives), skipping meals and/or excessive exercise in order to compensate for the binge eating.

- *Binge eating disorder* – This involves frequent binge eating without efforts to compensate for the binge in any way.

- *Body dysmorphic disorder* – This involves thinking obsessively about an appearance 'flaw' or 'defect' that is only slight or doesn't actually exist, and performing repetitive behaviours (e.g. checking, hiding or fixing) or repetitive mental acts (e.g. comparing self to others) for hours every day in order to feel better about the slight or non-existent flaw. Significant distress or negative impacts upon life are experienced as a result.

- *Muscle dysmorphia* – This involves a fear of being too thin or not muscular enough and can be accompanied by behaviours to hide actual body size, to avoid situations where actual body size will be seen by others and to improve muscle tone, such as excessive weight lifting, excessive use of protein shakes, steroid use and pectoral implants.

Other impacts that you may have also mentioned are that a negative body image can:

- have negative effects on a person's *self-esteem*
- lead some people to try and *cope* with their body image issues *in negative ways*, such as drinking, drug abuse and self-harming
- lead some people to feel like their life is not worth living and to *having thoughts about harming themselves*.

In the *Relationships* box, you may have talked about the stresses, pressures and strains that can occur in our relationships with others when we have a negative body image – for example, as a result of:

- the other person's worry for us
- us withdrawing from interacting socially with other people
- taking out our anger and frustration on others around us.

In the *Social and Leisure Activities* box, you may have talked about the impacts of avoiding social and leisure situations because of body image issues, which can include missing out on opportunities for:

- enjoyment
- achievement
- social interaction.

In the *Studies and Work* box, you may have talked about:

- a person's performance in their studies or at work reducing because of their inability to concentrate properly due to obsessive thoughts about their body
- a person falling behind in their studies because of missing school or college due to their body image concerns
- a person having to be home schooled because they cannot face leaving the house.

In the *Goals for the Future* box, you may have talked about how the impacts in all of the areas above can combine to have major impacts on a person's:

- motivation to achieve their future goals and desires

- ability to achieve them.

Although this chapter has shown you the negative impacts that can occur when we get stuck in a vicious cycle of negative body image, please don't be disheartened! It's possible to break out of this vicious cycle and banish your Body Image Thief for good! And the next few chapters will show you how.

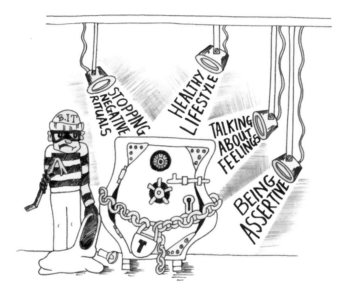

Banish Your Body Image Thief

An Introduction

So far, by progressing through this workbook, you have completed the following steps towards breaking out of the vicious cycle of negative body image, banishing your Body Image Thief and improving your body image:

- Step 1 – Understanding what body image is
- Step 2 – Understanding more about your own body image
- Step 3 – Realising that you are not on your own in experiencing body image issues
- Step 4 – Understanding how body image develops
- Step 5 – Understanding what influences your body image
- Step 6 – Understanding your body image-related thoughts
- Step 7 – Understanding your body image-related feelings
- Step 8 – Understanding your body image-related behaviours
- Step 9 – Understanding the negative impacts that negative body image can have.

The next steps are:

- Step 10 – Identifying what you want to change about how you think, feel and act in relation to your body
- Step 11 – Considering what having a positive body image will be like once you achieve it
- Step 12 – Showing yourself compassion.

Let's look at each of these steps.

Identifying what you want to change

Based on everything you have learnt so far about your body image, list in the next Body Image Box what things you would like to change about how you think, feel and act in relation to your body.

BODY IMAGE BOX

What I want to change

Considering what a positive body image would be like

For some people, the idea of having a positive body image is scary. This is because a negative body image is all they know, whereas a positive body image is the unknown. To help combat this fear of the unknown, write down as many words and phrases as you can to describe what you think having a positive body image will be like in the Body Image Box below. If you wish, you can even write a story or a poem or draw a picture to highlight what you think a positive body image would be like!

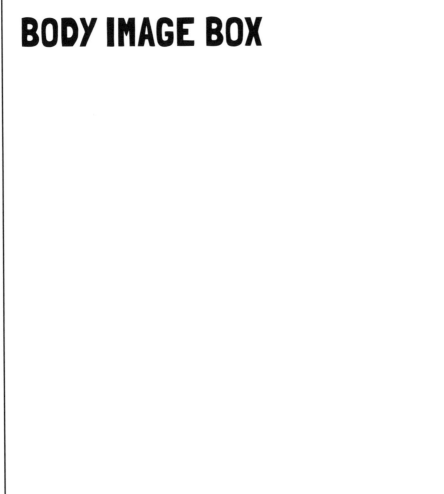

BODY IMAGE BOX

What will having a positive body image be like?

Here are some descriptions of positive body image that other young people gave:

And the following is a poem from another young person about having a positive body image.

A POSITIVE BODY IMAGE – WHAT IS THAT?

I can imagine it in my mind
But it's like a mirage to me
Always in the distance
But never reachable

But I believe that one day I will reach it
And that it will be a state of bliss
Because I will be content when I look in the mirror
And be happy to be me

I will be free to do what I please
Without fear or worry
About people calling me names
Or laughing and staring

I know the steps I need to take to get there
Will be tough and scary at times
The journey will be up and down
And I may want to quit

But if for the first time in my life I believe in me
Then I might just reach that mirage
And learn for myself how it feels
To be positive about my body
By Catherine, aged 15 years

Showing yourself compassion

You have always had the power to banish your Body Image Thief and improve your body image, but until you picked up this workbook, you may not have known how. So instead, you have acted in ways that seemed best at the time, including avoiding, hiding, checking and fixing. Even though they haven't actually helped in the long term, you did the best you could at the time and no-one can ever judge you or criticise you for that. And you shouldn't judge or criticise yourself for it either.

Q. If one of your friends was struggling to cope with something in their life, which of the following would you do? Tick which answer applies to you.

a) Criticise them ☐

b) Show them understanding and support ☐

I'm guessing you chose the understanding and support option and you would be right to do so. And this understanding and support is what we mean when we talk about compassion. So why not show yourself this same compassion? It's OK to struggle sometimes. You are not on your own in doing so, as an earlier chapter in this book showed you. And you are not a failure if you do. And you shouldn't beat yourself up about it if you do.

By understanding that it's OK to struggle sometimes, by showing yourself compassion and by letting go of the urges to criticise yourself for the situation you have ended up in, you will free yourself up to focus on the last two steps towards improving your body image, which are:

- Step 13 – Managing your thoughts
- Step 14 – Managing your behaviours.

Q. So why is it that these are the last two steps in improving your body image?

Because building positive body image isn't about changing how you look, it's about changing how you think about how you look and changing your behaviours as a result. Positive body image is based on how you think about your body, which is then reinforced by how you act. And you have A CHOICE TO CHANGE HOW YOU THINK AND HOW YOU ACT.

- You can make a choice to start THINKING IN REALISTIC AND ACCEPTING AND POSITIVE WAYS about your body and in response to appearance-related situations.

- And if you do, you are then more likely to start FEELING MORE POSITIVELY towards your body.

- As a result, you are filling your BODY IMAGE VAULT WITH THESE POSITIVE, ACCEPTING AND REALISTIC THOUGHTS AND FEELINGS.

And do you remember that one of the *Vault's special features* was *a dark, dusty, cobwebby corner where unwanted thoughts and feelings could be dumped*? Well, that's where you can push the no-longer-wanted unrealistic and overly negative thoughts too! In the next Body Image Box, have a go at drawing this corner of your Vault!

BODY IMAGE BOX

The dark, dusty, cobwebby corner of my Body Image Vault

You are then more likely to start BEHAVING IN CONSTRUCTIVE WAYS towards your body.

This then allows *your Vault's defence system to mend itself*. It repairs its broken locks and chains and replaces the bulbs that blew in its security lights. Your Vault will once again develop an amazingly effective defence system that protects all your realistic and positive thoughts and feelings and stops your Body Image Thief from being able to break in!

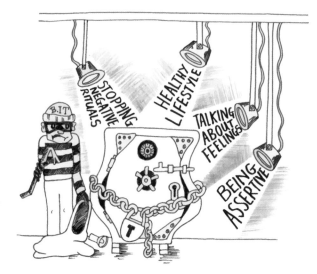

The result is...

your Body Image Thief is banished

and

your body image becomes positive!

And this really is possible, as the following stories show. Let's meet two 16-year-old identical twins, Michelle and Sarah, who both dislike the shape of their nose – which is obviously identical!

MICHELLE'S STORY

Michelle believes, 'My nose is so horrible that no-one will ever think I'm pretty, and as a result my life will never be how I want it to be!' Michelle spends a lot of time prodding at her nose while looking in the mirror, comparing her nose to the noses of people she believes are attractive and searching online for information on rhinoplasty (cosmetic nose surgery). When she is talking to people she tries to position herself in ways that make the shape of her nose less obvious and often tries to hide it with her hand. Michelle has a negative body image and it has many negative effects on her life. Michelle wants things to be different, but she believes that the only thing that will help to solve the problem is for her to have cosmetic surgery on her nose when she turns 18.

SARAH'S STORY

Sarah used to think and act in very similar ways to Michelle. However, because her negative body image was having so many negative impacts upon her and her life, Sarah decided to speak to a counsellor about her body image concerns. Sarah learnt that she could change how she thought about her nose and about her appearance in general. Sarah now believes that she is 'more than just my nose'. Sarah learnt over time to gradually stop poking and prodding at her nose and staring at it in the mirror. She accepts her nose as it is now and realises that it isn't worth worrying about. Sarah goes about her everyday life as normal and very rarely thinks about her nose any more. Sarah's body image has become positive.

Q. What is it that leads Sarah to have a positive body image and Michelle to have a negative one?

....
....
....

   A. Their thoughts and behaviours!

I know that trying to act and think differently will seem scary at first and I know it might even increase your worries and distress at first. But if you don't try to make these changes you will remain stuck in the vicious cycle of negative body image. As the following saying goes:

'If you always do what you have always done, you will always get what you have always got!'

So let's get started with doing something different! Let's manage your thoughts!

11

Banish Your Body Image Thief

Managing Your Thoughts and Beliefs

In this chapter, we will look at how you can manage your thoughts in order to banish your Body Image Thief and improve your body image. This is Step 13 in improving your body image and involves:

- accepting that thoughts are only thoughts

- challenging thinking errors in your everyday thoughts

- challenging your unrealistic and overly negative deeper beliefs.

Accepting that thoughts are only thoughts

Do you remember that I told you a little bit about mindfulness in the Introduction to this workbook? What I said was that when we practise mindfulness we make a choice to:

- become AWARE of our thoughts and feelings in the here and now

- ACCEPT our thoughts and feelings as they are, without criticising or judging them or ourselves or viewing them as reality

- LET negative thoughts and feelings GO instead of focusing on them over and over and over again.

So how can all this help with improving your body image and banishing your Body Image Thief?

Well, mindfulness teaches us that we have the power to let go of the thoughts that are bothering us when we are stuck in the vicious cycle of negative body image. We can do this by becoming aware of them in the here and now and accepting them for what they truly are – just thoughts. Thoughts cannot harm us; not unless we let them. Thus, it's how we choose to respond to them that matters. We can choose to view our thoughts as reality (i.e. as a truth that has to be believed in). Or we can choose to view them as what they really are (i.e. thoughts and only thoughts) and let them go!

In the Body Image Box below, write down one overly negative or unrealistic thought that you regularly have in relation to your body and then write down what you need to accept about it.

BODY IMAGE BOX

MY THOUGHT IS...	WHAT I NEED TO ACCEPT ABOUT MY THOUGHT IS...

The following Body Image Box shows how Harry, aged 13 years, completed the same task based on one of his thoughts about his body.

BODY IMAGE BOX

MY THOUGHT IS…	WHAT I NEED TO ACCEPT ABOUT MY THOUGHT IS…
I am unattractive	Just because I have a thought that I am unattractive doesn't mean that I am. Just because I'm thinking it doesn't make it fact.

Now let's move on to the next method of managing your thoughts.

Challenging thinking errors in your everyday thoughts

In Chapter 6 you identified the types of body image-related thinking errors that you often have in your everyday thoughts that help to keep you in the vicious cycle of negative body image. However, it is possible to challenge these thinking errors to help you to fill your Body Image Vault with more realistic everyday thoughts, banish your Body Image Thief and improve your body image. Here's how!

In order to challenge your thinking errors you need to use something called…

realistic thinking.

Realistic thinking involves doing what a scientist or detective would do, namely testing your thoughts out against the evidence. To do this, you can ask yourself questions like:

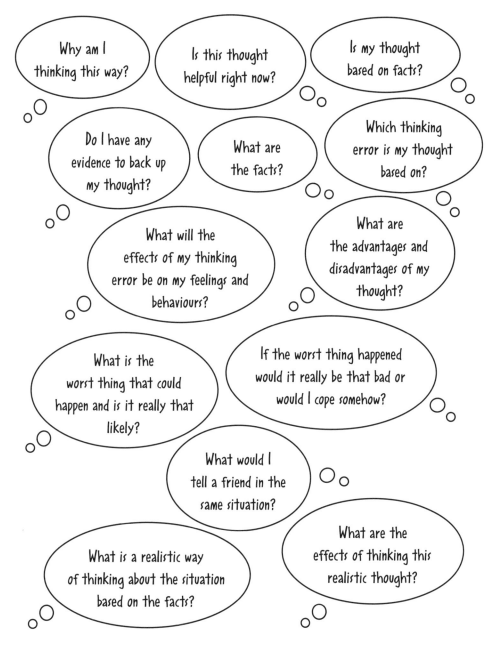

To practise challenging your thoughts in this way, answer the questions in the Body Image Box below based on a recent body image-related thinking error that you have had. See Chapter 6 as a reminder of thinking errors to help you complete this activity.

BODY IMAGE BOX

The situation was:

....

My thought was:

....

....

This involved the following type of thinking error:

....

A more realistic thought is:

....

....

So whenever you find yourself falling into the thinking error trap, try to think about the situation realistically based on the facts. Make sure you aren't being overly negative in some way or blowing things out of proportion. Remember, situations are normally not as bad as we think they are going to be, and even if our worst-case scenario actually occurs, we can normally find some way to cope with it, learn from it and move on from it.

Let's look at an example scenario to help you get some more practice at doing this. Do you remember Gary from Chapter 8 who wanted to avoid going to school swimming lessons? The following is a reminder of Gary's story.

GARY'S STORY

Gary is 10 years old. It is time for him to start school swimming lessons. Gary wants to learn to swim as he wants to join the Navy when he gets older. However, he avoids going for the first three weeks by pretending to be ill on those days. Gary believes he will look fat and ugly in his swimming shorts, that everyone in his class will laugh at him and that his school life will be awful from that point forward. So avoiding the lessons is the only thing Gary can think to do.

Q. What is Gary thinking?

....
....
....

Q. Is Gary making any thinking errors? If so, which one(s)?

....
....
....

Q. What thoughts could Gary let go of and send to the dark, cobwebby corner of his Body Image Vault?

....
....
....

Q. What realistic thoughts could Gary have?

....
....
....

Some people find it easier to challenge their thoughts by writing them down, especially in the initial stages. This allows you to use these notes again in the future if you have similar thoughts. The alternative thoughts worksheet below will help you with this. It will help you to start filling your Body Image Vault with more realistic thoughts, which in turn will help you to develop a more positive body image and banish your Body Image Thief!

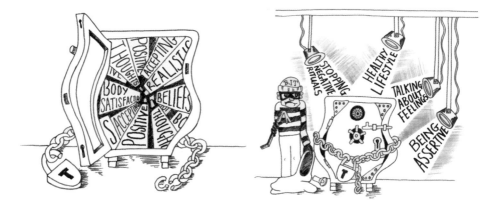

ALTERNATIVE THOUGHTS WORKSHEET

What is the situation?

....
....
....

What am I thinking?

....
....
....

Do my thoughts contain any of the following thinking errors? Highlight or colour in any that apply.

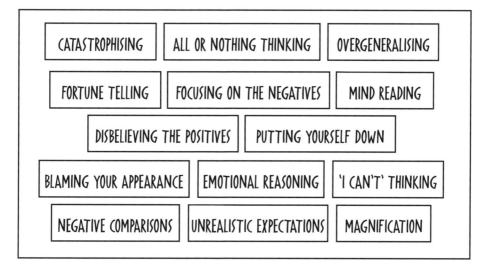

CATASTROPHISING	ALL OR NOTHING THINKING	OVERGENERALISING
FORTUNE TELLING	FOCUSING ON THE NEGATIVES	MIND READING
DISBELIEVING THE POSITIVES	PUTTING YOURSELF DOWN	
BLAMING YOUR APPEARANCE	EMOTIONAL REASONING	'I CAN'T' THINKING
NEGATIVE COMPARISONS	UNREALISTIC EXPECTATIONS	MAGNIFICATION

What facts and evidence do I need to be aware of?

....

....

....

Are my thoughts based on these facts and evidence? Tick which answer applies to you.

a) Yes ☐   b) No ☐

If not, how can I think more realistically based on these facts and evidence in order to banish my Body Image Thief?

....

....

....

Challenging your unrealistic and overly negative deeper beliefs

Once you have practised challenging the thinking errors in your everyday thoughts, it is time to start challenging any similar distortions in your deeper beliefs. Challenging unrealistic and overly negative deeper beliefs involves:

- identifying what your deeper beliefs are

- assessing which are unrealistic or overly negative

- developing alternative, more realistic beliefs based on evidence.

IDENTIFYING WHAT YOUR DEEPER BELIEFS ARE

You completed an activity in Chapter 6 where you were asked to identify your body image-related deeper beliefs. However, you may have struggled to do this at that point. If so, don't worry. Try looking through copies of the alternative thoughts worksheet that you have filled out for your everyday thoughts, and see if you can see any overarching themes or patterns to these thoughts. If you can, these will be your deeper beliefs. Also go back to the example list of deeper beliefs that I provided in Chapter 6 for help too and re-write your list of deeper beliefs in the next Body Image Box.

BODY IMAGE BOX

My deeper beliefs

ASSESSING WHICH DEEPER BELIEFS ARE UNREALISTIC OR OVERLY NEGATIVE

In order to assess which of your deeper beliefs are unrealistic or overly negative you need to use the same realistic thinking approach that you took for the thinking errors. So, in a nutshell, you need to assess the evidence. Again you can ask yourself a range of questions to help you test your beliefs, including:

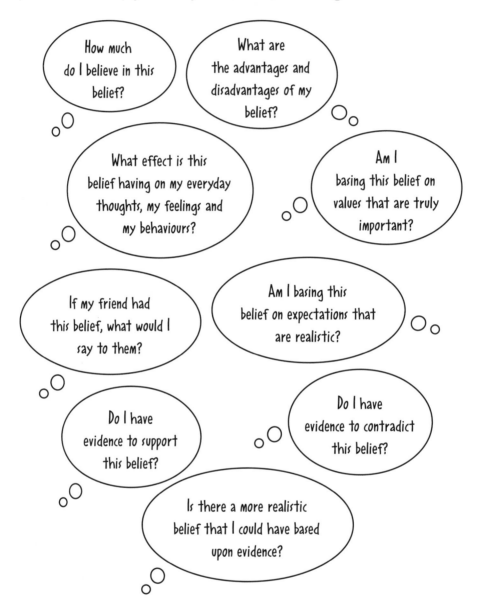

How much do I believe in this belief?

What are the advantages and disadvantages of my belief?

What effect is this belief having on my everyday thoughts, my feelings and my behaviours?

Am I basing this belief on values that are truly important?

If my friend had this belief, what would I say to them?

Am I basing this belief on expectations that are realistic?

Do I have evidence to support this belief?

Do I have evidence to contradict this belief?

Is there a more realistic belief that I could have based upon evidence?

The following deeper beliefs worksheet can help you with assessing your beliefs and with developing new ones to fill your Body Image Vault with. Try completing the questions in this worksheet for each of your deeper beliefs that you believe need challenging.

DEEPER BELIEFS WORKSHEET

My existing deeper belief is:

....

The evidence that supports this belief is:

....
....

The evidence that contradicts this belief is:

....
....

An alternative deeper belief could be:

....

Which is the most realistic? Tick which answer applies to you.

    a) Old belief   ☐   b) New belief   ☐

Which belief helps to banish my Body Image Thief? Tick which answer applies to you.

    a) Old belief   ☐   b) New belief   ☐

Here is an example of a deeper beliefs worksheet that Gary, aged 10, completed.

GARY'S DEEPER BELIEFS WORKSHEET

My existing deeper belief is:

I am fat and ugly.

The evidence that supports this belief is:

I think I look fat and ugly when I wear swimming shorts.

The evidence that contradicts this belief is:

- No-one has ever laughed at me when wearing swimming shorts before.
- No-one has ever called me names because of how I look.
- No-one has ever told me I am fat and ugly.
- My mum tells me I'm not fat.
- A girl at school said she liked me.

An alternative deeper belief could be:

I am a worthy person no matter what I weigh.

Which is the most realistic?

b) New belief

Which belief helps to banish my Body Image Thief?

b) New belief

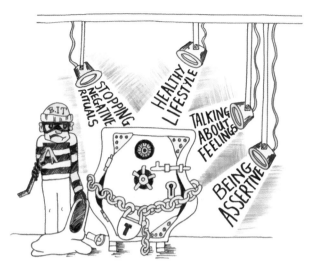

DEVELOPING ALTERNATIVE DEEPER BELIEFS BASED UPON EVIDENCE

As stated earlier in the chapter, your existing deeper beliefs have been very likely influenced by some of the factors that we looked at in Chapter 5. Thus, in order to help you with your quest to develop more realistic beliefs, it can be helpful to think about the following points.

- 'Ideal' body types are unrealistic.
- We all look different.
- It's OK for our bodies to change.
- Our appearance is not the problem.
- We don't know what other people are thinking.
- We are all more than just our appearance.
- Should appearance be our number one value?

'Ideal' body types are unrealistic

As you saw in Chapter 5, we see and hear lots of messages about 'ideal' body types from a variety of sources, including photographs in magazines and in advertisements.

I would like you to look through either a printed or online magazine and answer the questions in the Becoming Media Savvy! box below.

BECOMING MEDIA SAVVY!

Q1. What kinds of images does the magazine contain of men and women?

....

....

Q2. What kinds of words does it use to describe male and female appearance?

....

....

Q3. Are there any images or articles that criticise celebrities based on how they look?

....

....

Q4. Why do you think the media uses these kinds of images, words and articles?

....

....

Q5. What messages is it sending out about male and female body types?

....

....

Q6. How do you think and feel in response to these messages?

....

....

Q7. How do you want to act in response to these messages?

....

....

Q8. How often do you see your body type in the magazine and how do you think and feel as a result?

....

....

Q9. How many of the images have been digitally altered in your opinion?

....

....

Q10. Does knowing that the images are digitally altered affect how you think and feel in response to the images?

....

....

Q11. Do you think the images in the magazine accurately represent body types in society?

....

....

By looking through the magazine and answering the questions in the 'Becoming Media Savvy!' activity, you will have no doubt noticed that photographs don't always provide an accurate record of what is before them. Images can be altered in a variety of ways. In fact, we rarely see an image that hasn't been altered in some way in magazines and adverts today. And as a result, the gap between 'ideal' images and 'real' people is getting wider and wider, and it has become impossible for the majority of the population to meet these ideals.

Let's take a look at some of the digital alteration techniques that are used regularly today by the media and advertising industries.

- *Airbrushing* – This is where techniques are used to smooth out imperfections, such as spots or moles.

- *Digital enhancement* – This is where parts of an image are enhanced in some way, such as making hair fuller or shinier, making muscles more defined, making teeth whiter, etc.

- *Digital manipulation* – This is where an image is altered in a more drastic way, such as changing the model's body shape or the shape of their facial features. Sometimes a body part of the model is replaced with the same body part from another model.

- *Use of lighting* – Special lighting positions can be used when the picture is being taken to highlight certain areas of the model's body and hide others.

We need to become more aware of these forms of alteration in images so that we can realise that we are judging ourselves against standards that are NOT REAL! What you are looking at in that photograph is unlikely to be an accurate representation of what the model actually looks like. Plus we have to remember that these aren't the only reasons why the images in the media and in adverts don't reflect how people look in general in society.

Q. List how many types of people you think are likely to be involved in helping a celebrity or model look the way they do for a photo shoot or to appear on TV or in a film.

....
....
....
....
....
....
....
....

The model or celebrity will have gone through hours of hair and make-up, had clothes chosen specifically to enhance his/her shape and may have even had surgical enhancements. And many photos will have been taken before a photo is selected for use.

Thus, the physical attributes that we are trying to achieve aren't actually real! We may as well be comparing ourselves to fictional characters in a book! There is nothing wrong with wanting to look attractive. But we need to realise that if we put expectations on ourselves that are unachievable and unrealistic we are setting ourselves up to be critical of the way we look and to feel distressed, anxious, down, angry and so on as a result. And remember, the media, advertising, beauty, fashion and fitness industries may be plugging the myth that there is an ideal size, but if we listen to it, we are the ones buying into it and keeping that myth going! Societal messages and expectations can't hurt us unless we let them!

To learn more about digital alterations of images in the media and in advertising, go to www.dove.ca/en/Tips-Topics-And-Tools/ Videos/Evolution.aspx and watch the video called 'Evolution'.

Here are two more activities about 'ideal' body images for you to try. You can pick the one you prefer or you can even have a go at both! The choice is yours!

YOUR VOICE!

Think about the different types of industries that benefit from us thinking our bodies aren't 'perfect'. Write a letter to a company from one of these industries with your opinion on the messages they are sending out about body image, the impacts it may be having on young people today and how they can improve this.

PRODUCE AN ADVERT!

Find an advert in a magazine that uses 'ideal' body images or messages about 'ideal' body types as a way of selling its product or service. Now write down or draw ideas for an alternative advert for the same product or service that will still encourage people to buy the product or service but that doesn't use 'ideal' body imagery.

We all look different

Q. What do you think it would be like to live on this planet with everyone looking the same?

....

....

....

All of us are different and unique in many ways, including in terms of our bodies. Human bodies come in a variety of shapes and sizes and this is normal. It is genetics at work.

So even if we all ate the same amount of the same things and did the same amount of the same type of exercise over the same period of time, we wouldn't all look the same. There would still be variations in our body shape, size and weight because the genetics we inherit determine our basic body structure, such as the size of our skeleton, the development of our muscles and, to a certain extent, the amount and location of fat throughout our body.

Because of this, comparisons with other people, especially digitally altered photographs of people, are actually irrelevant! And because of this, no one size is actually 'ideal'. And only a minority of males and females are genetically programmed to meet 'ideal' body types! In addition to this, no-one is perfect. We all have our flaws and this is OK and normal too! We need to learn to focus on the things that we like about our bodies instead of just focusing on what we believe to be our 'imperfections'. Here are some activities to help you with this!

In the next Body Image Box, write down at least three things you like about your body and why. Then write down at least three positive statements about your body. We call these...

positive affirmations.

Millie, aged 11, came up with the following positive affirmations about her body:

'I am beautiful just the way I am.'

'I am me, and that's just fine.'

'I have a pretty face.'

BODY IMAGE BOX

Things I like about my body and why:

....
....
....
....
....
....
....
....
....
....
....
....
....
....

My positive affirmations about my body:

....
....
....
....
....
....
....
....
....
....
....
....
....
....

If it feels comfortable for you to do so, try having a go at the following activities in front of the mirror.

MIRROR ACTIVITIES

DAY 1

Look in the mirror and describe:

- what you see
- what thoughts go through your head
- how you feel emotionally.

You are likely to find that you focus on the aspects of your body that you dislike. Instead of just observing them, you are likely to criticise them and think about them in negative ways. This is likely to make you feel negative emotions and may lead you to think about behaving in certain ways.

DAY 2

Today, do the same mirror gazing exercise. However, this time, look at your body generally as a whole for a minute and then objectively describe each part to yourself without judgments and interpretations. For example, 'my eyes are blue'. Be aware of how you feel when you do this. At the end think about what you have learnt from this activity and write it down below.

Here's another activity for you to try!

CELEBRATE DIFFERENT BODIES!

Produce a:

- short story
- poem
- song or rap
- blog
- dance piece
- play
- drawing
- poster
- photograph(s)

...that celebrate diversity in human appearance. Write your ideas down below and then produce it on your computer or on separate pieces of paper.

It's OK for our bodies to change

HOW YOU HAVE CHANGED!

Find photographs of yourself as a baby, toddler, young child, etc. Then write down below how you have changed physically and what the good things about these changes are.

It is normal for our bodies to change in many different ways through our lifetime. One of these stages of change is puberty. Puberty usually happens between the ages of 8 and 14 years. But some young people can begin puberty earlier or later than these ages. During puberty your body releases hormones that trigger changes in your body that indicate you are developing into a teenager and eventually into an adult. Not everyone experiences these changes at the same rate.

For girls, these changes include:

- height increase
- body hair growing under arms and in pubic area
- breast development
- acne
- period begins
- increase in body fat
- increase in body curves
- fuller hips
- oily hair and skin.

For boys, these changes include:

- height increase
- body hair growing on face, under arms and in genitals area
- acne
- decrease in body fat
- increase in muscle
- oily hair and skin
- penis and testicles increase in size
- voice breaks.

Our appearance is not the problem

A common belief held by people with a negative body image is that their appearance is causing all their problems. However, as you have learnt, there is a difference between our body image and our actual appearance. It is how we think, feel and act towards how we look that determines if we have a positive or negative body image, not how we actually look. No matter what your physical description, you can have either a positive or a negative body image, and just because you may have the 'ideal' body in someone else's eyes it doesn't mean you have a positive body image. Jake's story on the next page highlights this.

JAKE'S STORY

Jake is an 18-year-old celebrity male with a body that is admired by millions of females worldwide and the envy of men across the globe. But despite this, Jake isn't happy with his appearance. All Jake notices when he looks in the mirror is his height. Jake believes he is 'shorter than a man should be' and that no matter how muscular his physique he will 'never make up for my height'.

We don't know what other people are thinking

Unless you have mindreading super powers, you actually have no idea what other people are thinking about you and your appearance. And yet, we often worry about what other people think and predict what they are thinking at times – the 'mindreading' thinking error. But worrying will only bring us negative impacts and we will never know if what we predict someone is thinking is true unless they tell us.

Remember, other people rarely judge you as harshly as you judge yourself – we are normally our own worst critics. Go online to www.youtube.com/watch?v=XpaOjMXyJGk and have a look at the video 'Dove Beauty Sketches', as it shows women describing themselves to a sketch artist and then a stranger describing them to a sketch artist. The stranger's descriptions are more positive and accurate!

We are all more than just our appearance

It is vital we realise that we are more than just our appearance. We cannot define ourselves solely on how we look, as our bodies are just one part of us.

A PICTURE TELLS A THOUSAND WORDS – OR DOES IT?

Take a photograph of yourself or look at a recent photograph of yourself. Does this show who you are as a person or is this just a snapshot of how you look for a brief moment in time?

Your personal characteristics, your talents, your skills and your achievements are just as much a part of you as your physical appearance. And although societal messages are keen to convey the importance of appearance to being liked and loved, what actually counts more is the kind of person you are.

In the next Body Image Box draw an outline of a human body. Around the outside of the body, write down the kinds of things a person can tell about you just by looking at you. On the inside write down the kinds of things a person can find out about you by getting to know you.

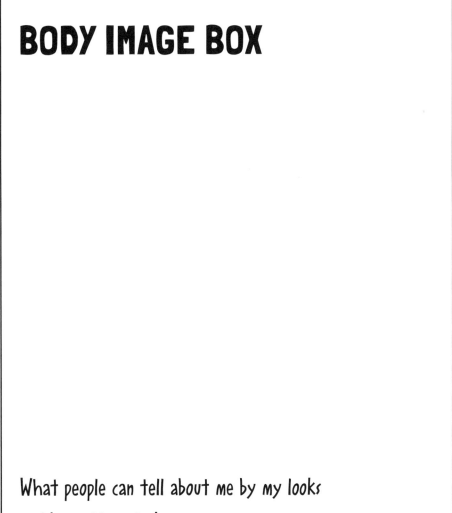

BODY IMAGE BOX

What people can tell about me by my looks
and by getting to know me

Q. Which things are more important to you? Tick which answer applies to you.

a) Those around the outside of the body ☐

b) Those on the inside of the body ☐

Now think for a minute about one of your close friends. What is it that you like about them? List these things in the Body Image Box below.

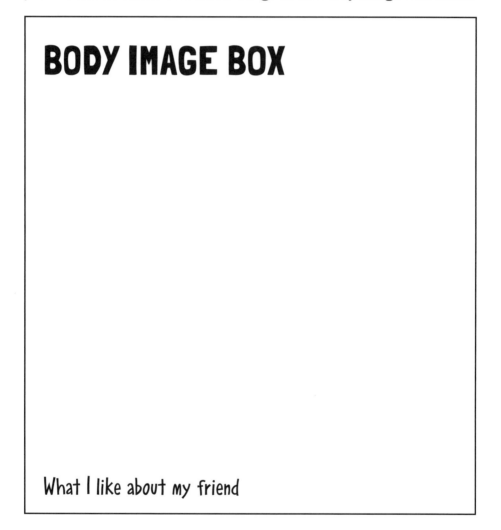

BODY IMAGE BOX

What I like about my friend

I'm guessing that what you have listed focuses on who they are as a person, not how they look. Now think about a person that you admire. Write down in the next Body Image Box what you admire about that person.

BODY IMAGE BOX

The person I admire is:

....

The things that I admire about that person are:

....

....

....

....

....

....

....

....

....

....

....

....

....

....

....

....

....

....

Again, I'm guessing that what you have listed focuses on who they are as a person, not how they look. So why is it that we focus so much on appearance when it comes to ourselves? Why is it that we have beliefs and thoughts that revolve around appearance being vital to whether we are a worthy person, whether people will like us and whether we will be happy and successful in life?

Q. If your friend had a flaw in their appearance, would you like them any less? Tick which answer applies to you.

a) Yes ☐   b) No ☐

Q. If the person you admire had a flaw in their appearance, would you admire them any less? Tick which answer applies to you.

a) Yes □   b) No □

I'm sure your answers to these questions are no. So why do we set different standards for ourselves?

We all have weaknesses or flaws or limitations. This is normal. But if we focus on them and ignore the rest of who we are as a person, then we aren't being fair to ourselves. What we need to learn from this is to put our flaws into perspective and to put our appearance into perspective by focusing on ourselves as a whole, not just on one aspect of ourselves. Think about your personal characteristics, qualities and traits, think about your skills and talents, and think about the things you have achieved in life. They all make up who you are as a person as well. It's not about looking at yourself through rose-tinted glasses for the sake of it. It's about looking at yourself positively based on what is factual and therefore realistic. By recognising all these other aspects of yourself, you will learn to place less importance on appearance as a determining factor in your self-worth and by doing so you will be able to:

- fill your Body Image Vault with more realistic, positive and accepting thoughts and feelings

- improve your body image

- banish your Body Image Thief!

Here are some activities to help you to do this.

In the next Body Image Box, list ten positive things about yourself and write down a piece of evidence to back up each statement. To give you an example of what I mean, here are two things that Susie, aged 14 years, said about herself with accompanying evidence.

'I am a funny person because my friends always laugh at my jokes.'

'I am a good artist because I won an art competition last year.'

BODY IMAGE BOX

POSITIVES ABOUT ME	SUPPORTING EVIDENCE

Now list at least three things you have achieved in your life so far and write down at least one positive thing that each achievement shows you about yourself in the following Body Image Box.

BODY IMAGE BOX

MY ACHIEVEMENTS	POSITIVE THINGS THEY SHOW ABOUT ME

Q. Was it your appearance that led you to these successes in your life or was it other qualities about you as a person? Tick which answer applies to you.

a) My appearance   ☐   b) Other qualities   ☐

Next write down at least five strengths that you think you have that can help you to face situations in life in the Body Image Box below.

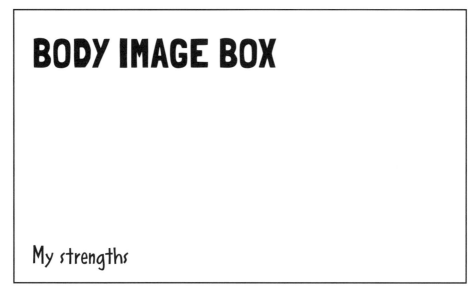

Now write down at least three things you believe you are good at in the next Body Image Box.

Finally, based on everything you've come up with so far, write down five positive statements about yourself in the next Body Image Box. Remember, we call these positive affirmations. To help you with this, here are Susie's positive affirmations:

'I am a creative person.'

'I am a talented person.'

'I am a good person.'

'I am a good friend.'

'I am a supportive person.'

BODY IMAGE BOX

My positive affirmations

Thinking about all the positive and realistic things about yourself in this way will help you to contradict your unrealistic and overly negative deeper beliefs and help you to develop more positive and realistic ones. This will in turn help you to banish your Body Image Thief!

Below is another activity to help you to realise that you are more than just your appearance. Imagine you are 75 years old. In the Body Image Box below, write down what kinds of memories you want to be able to look back on and how you want people to think about the kind of person you have been throughout your life.

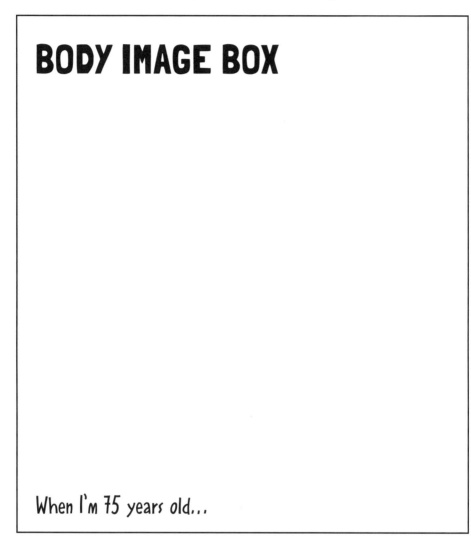

BODY IMAGE BOX

When I'm 75 years old...

Should appearance be our number one value?

Q. What is more important? Tick which answer applies to you.

    a) To be a good person ☐

    b) To be a physically attractive person ☐

Q. Can physical attractiveness guarantee you happiness? Tick which answer applies to you.

    a) Yes   ☐   b) No   ☐

Many people today view their appearance as more important than their health or their future goals or achievements. But this is leading to all the negative impacts that we have seen in earlier chapters. To overcome this, we need to develop alternative values. Our values are things that we view as important in the way we live our lives. They are the factors that we measure the success and happiness of our lives by.

Felix, aged 15, has the following values:

'I see being a good friend as important.'

'I see being healthy as important.'

'I see being successful in my future career as important.'

'I see passing my exams as important.'

'I see being emotionally calm and happy as important.'

Here is an activity to help you come up with a set of values for yourself. In the next Body Image Box list any values that you believe are important under any of the categories listed. If a category isn't relevant to you and your values, please just ignore it. Make sure you are including values that are truly important to you, not just because you think other people will approve of them.

BODY IMAGE BOX

Family values:

....

....

Friendship values:

....

....

Intimate relationship values:

....

....

Education values:

....

....

Leisure and social activities values:

....

....

Health values:

....

....

Mental and emotional health values:

....

....

Other values:

....

....

My values

I hope this activity will have revealed to you that there are many things in life that you value more than your appearance. Becoming aware of the importance of other values in this way can help you when you are developing new deeper beliefs.

All the activities in this chapter should have helped you to develop new deeper beliefs about appearance and to think about your body in more realistic, positive and accepting ways on a daily basis. Here is an activity that will help bring everything you have learnt together – thus helping you to banish your Body Image Thief!

MY SOURCES OF EVIDENCE

Create a scrapbook, box or journal that will be your source of evidence against any negative thoughts or beliefs that you have. This will also be your source of inspiration for thinking and feeling in more realistic and positive ways. It can really help to look at this on a regular basis, especially at times when you are struggling with your body image concerns. You can put the answers to the many activities in this workbook in there along with any of the following and anything else you want to include:

- quotes that inspire you
- photos of yourself that you like
- your positive body image playlist – songs that inspire you
- your positive body image reading list – books that inspire you
- your positive body image film list – films that inspire you
- adverts and images and articles that promote body diversity
- compliments that you've received
- mementos that remind you of times when you have felt body confident.

You have now learnt about all the different strategies that you can use to:

- challenge and dump overly negative and unrealistic thoughts and beliefs
- fill your Body Image Vault with more realistic, positive and accepting ones.

Write down your own managing thoughts goals in the next Body Image Box.

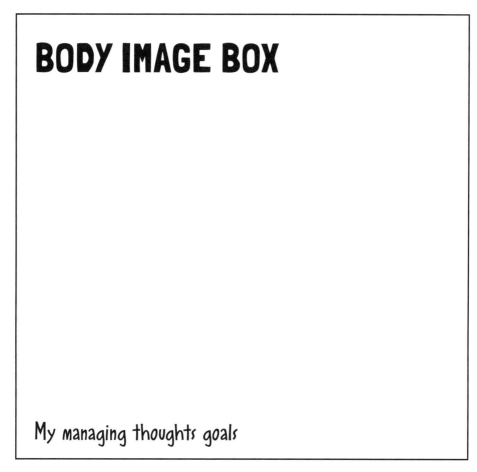

BODY IMAGE BOX

My managing thoughts goals

Good luck meeting these goals and banishing your Body Image Thief!

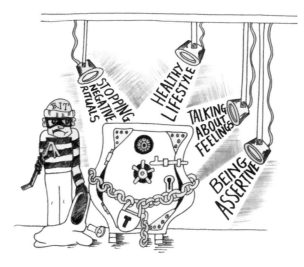

Banish Your Body Image Thief

Managing Your Behaviours

The important final step in banishing your Body Image Thief and improving your body image is to learn how to:

- manage your self-defeating behaviours
- implement constructive behaviours.

Managing self-defeating behaviours

Here we will look at:

- reducing avoidance and hiding
- reducing checking and fixing.

By working on reducing these behaviours, you will help your Body Image Vault's defence system to mend and you will be well on your way to banishing your Body Image Thief!

Reducing avoidance and hiding

In order to stop AVOIDANCE you need to face your fears, worries and distress by gradually putting yourself into the situations that you would normally avoid. Psychologists call this...

graded exposure.

The idea behind graded exposure is that if you stay in the situation that you would normally avoid for long enough your worry, fear or distress will gradually reduce until eventually it disappears completely. This allows you to see that there is a difference between how you think and feel about a situation and what actually happens in it. The best way to do this graded exposure is by using an...

exposure ladder.

Here's how to create an exposure ladder:

1. Write down the type of body image-related situation you get worried, fearful or distressed about.

2. Draw a ladder.

3. On the bottom rung of the ladder, place the first thing you want to do to confront your worry, fear or distress. This needs to be the action that you will find the easiest to do.

4. On the top rung put the final step that you want to achieve.

5. Put other gradual steps on the rungs in between.

6. Start to perform each action on your ladder, beginning with the action on the bottom rung.

7. Accept that you will feel some worry, fear or distress at first as that is normal, but remind yourself that it will pass.

8. Only move onto the next rung when you are ready to.

9. If you feel unable to do one of the actions, try breaking it down into smaller steps and tackle those bit by bit.

10. If you need to repeat a step several times until you feel completely comfortable with it, that is OK.

11. If you are struggling to motivate yourself to complete the steps on your ladder, remind yourself of why you need to, the benefits it will bring and that it will be OK.

12. Use the realistic thinking techniques that you learnt in the previous chapter along with other behavioural strategies that you will learn later in this chapter (e.g. relaxation techniques) to help you along the way.

13. Make a note of what helped you to get through each step in order to help you complete other steps on this ladder or on a different ladder.

14. Reward and praise yourself for achieving each step.

Here's an example of an exposure ladder for Gary, who we first met in Chapter 8.

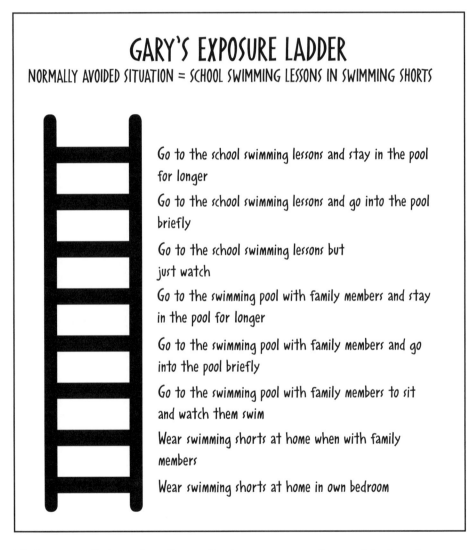

GARY'S EXPOSURE LADDER
NORMALLY AVOIDED SITUATION = SCHOOL SWIMMING LESSONS IN SWIMMING SHORTS

Go to the school swimming lessons and stay in the pool for longer

Go to the school swimming lessons and go into the pool briefly

Go to the school swimming lessons but just watch

Go to the swimming pool with family members and stay in the pool for longer

Go to the swimming pool with family members and go into the pool briefly

Go to the swimming pool with family members to sit and watch them swim

Wear swimming shorts at home when with family members

Wear swimming shorts at home in own bedroom

Pick one of the situations that you normally avoid due to your concerns about your body and design your own exposure ladder to address your avoidance in the next Body Image Box. Then try to gradually work your way through each step on the ladder. But don't use any other self-defeating behaviours as you complete the exposure, such as hiding behaviours, otherwise you will think you only achieved the steps on your exposure ladder because you used the hiding behaviours!

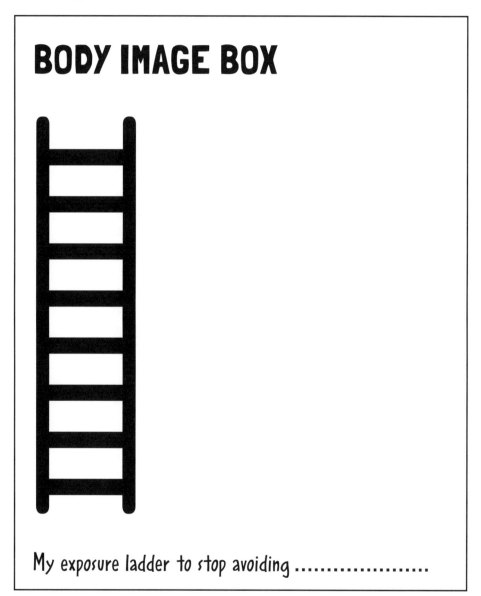

BODY IMAGE BOX

My exposure ladder to stop avoiding ....

Once you have successfully achieved all the steps, you can develop exposure ladders for other situations that you commonly avoid. But don't worry if a particular exposure situation feels too difficult at first – try preparing for it beforehand. The questions in the next Body Image Box can help you with this.

BODY IMAGE BOX

The exposure situation:

....

How I might be thinking:

....

....

How I might feel:

....

....

How I might want to behave:

....

....

How I can challenge any thoughts that might hinder me from completing the exposure:

....

....

How I can cope with any negative feelings during the exposure:

....

....

You can use the same exposure ladder and preparation questions to reduce your HIDING behaviours too. Just think about one of the ways you hide your body or part of your body and break that down into gradual steps for reducing that behaviour too! In the Body Image Box below, have a go at developing an exposure ladder for one of your hiding behaviours.

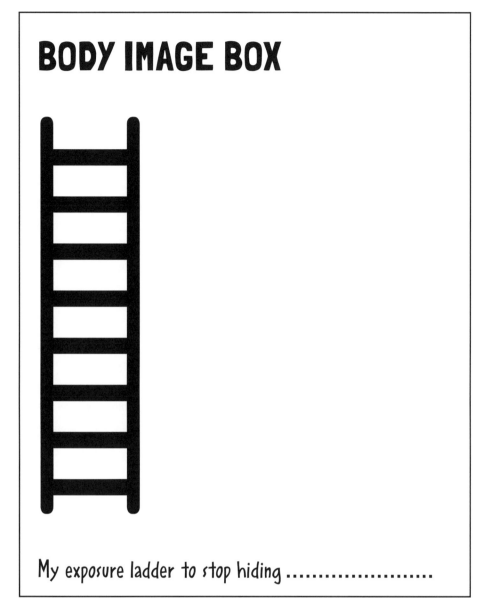

BODY IMAGE BOX

My exposure ladder to stop hiding ....

Completing graded exposure ladders like this will help you to mend your Vault's defence system and banish your Body Image Thief!

Reducing checking and fixing

So how do we reduce our CHECKING and FIXING behaviours in order to improve our body image? We do this by setting ourselves a gradual plan for reducing the frequency and amount of the checking and fixing that we do. This is what psychologists call...

response prevention.

They use this name because response prevention involves preventing yourself from responding to your worry or fear or distress with your usual rituals, in this case your checking and fixing behaviours.

So let's look at some of the strategies that you can use to reduce your checking and fixing behaviours.

DITCH THOSE TOOLS!

This involves reducing the opportunity to perform the behaviour by removing the tools you need (e.g. getting rid of your weighing scales) or restricting your access to the environment you need (e.g. leaving the bathroom when you have finished brushing your teeth instead of remaining there to pick your skin in front of the mirror).

DELAY, DELAY, DELAY!

This involves waiting a little while before you start to perform the behaviour, as by waiting, even for just five minutes, you can reduce the urge to perform this behaviour. You are showing yourself that you have a choice over whether and when you perform this behaviour.

SAY 'STOP!'

This involves saying a word such as 'stop!' to yourself when you feel the urge to perform the behaviour. This gives you the opportunity you need to assess your thoughts that are leading to the urge using the realistic thinking methods discussed in the previous chapter.

DISTRACT YOURSELF!

This involves using other activities as a way of distracting yourself from the urge to perform the behaviour. The best forms of distraction are things that you enjoy doing, things that give you a sense of achievement and things that really absorb your attention.

SET LIMITS!

This involves placing limits on your checking and fixing behaviours to restrict them in some way. This can include setting limits for the number of times you perform the behaviour in a day or a week or for the amount of time you spend performing the behaviour. It can also include only allowing yourself to perform the behaviour at a set time each day and if you miss that time you have to wait till the next day. And it can also involve only allowing yourself to perform the behaviour in response to certain situations and not others.

WORK THOSE MUSCLES DIFFERENTLY!

This involves performing any behaviour that uses the same muscle groups as the checking or fixing behaviour instead. Psychologists call this a 'competing action' because you can't do the two at once. Examples include squeezing a stress ball instead of pinching at your 'fat' or painting your garden fence instead of excessively brushing your hair.

RESISTANCE!

You can also resist the urge to perform the behaviour completely. You may be able to do this straight away for some of your less-frequent behaviours. But for behaviours that you have the strongest urge for, you may have to build up to this more gradually using some of the other techniques above.

You are likely to feel increased levels of worry or fear or distress at first when trying to reduce your checking and fixing behaviours in these ways. But this is normal and will gradually reduce. You can use some of the other techniques that I will discuss in the rest of this chapter to help you through this time, such as relaxation techniques. It can also help to prepare in advance by asking yourself similar preparation questions to those I suggested for the graded exposure.

In order for response prevention to work effectively you need to set yourself a plan with specific goals for reducing each checking or fixing behaviour. Here is an example plan for another young person.

BETH'S PLAN

Beth, aged 11 years, wants to reduce her excessive application of cleansers, toners and moisturisers on her face. So she came up with the following response prevention plan:

- Restrict myself to only applying my lotions four times a day at first.

- Then restrict myself to only applying my lotions twice a day – once at 7.30am before school and once at 9pm before bed.

- In the beginning, give my lotions to my mum to hide away from me between uses so I don't have access to them.

- Then stick to this restriction but have the lotions back in my room between uses.

- Use listening to my favourite music as a distraction if I feel the urge to use my lotions between these times.

In the next Body Image Box, develop a response prevention plan for one of your checking or fixing behaviours. And remember, response prevention helps you to mend your Body Image Vault's defence system and banish your Body Image Thief!

BODY IMAGE BOX

My response prevention plan

Now you know how to manage your self-defeating behaviours, let's look at how you can implement constructive behaviours. Doing so will protect your Body Image Vault and banish your Body Image Thief.

Implementing constructive behaviours

Constructive behaviours include:

- using relaxation and distraction techniques
- talking
- changing your body talk
- having fun and enjoyment
- being assertive
- living healthily
- focusing your attention.

You don't have to try and use them all. Just try those that are relevant to you and your body image symptoms. Let's start by looking at relaxation and distraction techniques.

Using relaxation and distraction techniques

You can use simple relaxation techniques, such as deep breathing exercises, to help you to relax when you're feeling worried or fearful or distressed by body image-related situations. These can be helpful when you are trying to face situations that you would normally avoid or when trying to reduce your hiding behaviours during the graded exposure as well as when trying to reduce your checking and fixing behaviours through response prevention as we discussed earlier in this chapter.

Have a go at the following exercises and see what you think. It's OK if these don't feel right to you as they aren't always suitable for everybody. But give them a go and see what you think. Remember, you can always try other forms of activity/exercise that are aimed at relaxation such as meditation, yoga and T'ai Chi.

DEEP BREATHING EXERCISE

Either sit down or lie down on your back. Focus on your breathing. Put one hand on your upper chest and one on your abdomen (just below your ribs). Gently breathe in, and as you do so, notice that your abdomen rises slowly under your hand. Slowly breathe out, noticing how your abdomen falls down slowly. Repeat the process, breathing in and out with a slow, steady rhythm. You are breathing correctly if your hand on your abdomen moves up and down slowly but the hand on your chest remains still.

RELAXATION EXERCISES

RELAXATION EXERCISE 1

Close your eyes and imagine yourself somewhere peaceful, happy or enjoyable — somewhere that makes you feel relaxed and happy. Focus on that image, start to build the detail, and for a short time imagine that you are actually there. Breathe deeply and slowly as you do.

RELAXATION EXERCISE 2

Focus on one muscle in your body at a time, and slowly tighten and then relax the muscle.

RELAXATION EXERCISE 3

Lie on your back. Breathe in deeply and slowly, imagining that the breath is coming in through the soles of your feet, travelling up through your body and exiting through your head. Breathe in again and this time imagine that the breath is coming in through your head, travelling down through your body and out through the soles of your feet. Repeat this exercise several times and slowly.

VISUALISATION EXERCISES

- Imagine a calming image.
- Imagine a funny image.
- Imagine you are in a happy place.
- Imagine your worries as visual things being discarded by you.
- Imagine yourself tackling a worrying situation and what it would look like and feel like.

Alternatively, you can use activities that you enjoy to help you relax. These same activities may also help to take your mind off the urge to check or fix. Have a go at coming up with relaxation and distraction activities that might work for you and write them down in the Body Image Box below.

BODY IMAGE BOX

Positive things I can do to relax:

....
....
....
....
....
....

Positive things I can do to distract myself:

....
....
....
....
....
....

Examples that you might have included in your list are:

- breathing and relaxation techniques
- exercise
- yoga or T'ai Chi
- meditation
- hot bath/shower
- listening to music
- watching TV
- spending time with friends or family
- volunteering
- extra-curricular/leisure activities
- going to the cinema
- reading.

Talking about your concerns

Talking about your body image concerns with a person that you trust is an important way to manage those concerns, as it can help you to:

| EXPRESS HOW YOU ARE FEELING | CHALLENGE YOUR THOUGHTS | IDENTIFY ALTERNATIVE WAYS TO COPE WITH SITUATIONS |

Q. Which of the following people do you think you could talk to?

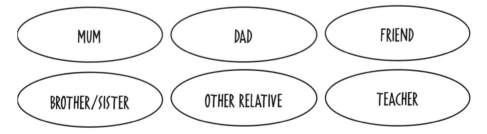

MUM   DAD   FRIEND

BROTHER/SISTER   OTHER RELATIVE   TEACHER

Q. Are there any other people who you would talk to who aren't mentioned in the previous question? If so, write them down below.

....

....

Don't forget, you can also talk to a professional, such as a doctor, psychologist or counsellor, about your body image concerns either face to face or through a telephone helpline. Remember, talking can help you to banish your Body Image Thief and improve your body image.

Changing your body talk

How you talk about your body needs to be realistic and positive, just like your thoughts, otherwise it can have negative impacts on your body image. Becoming more aware of how you talk about your body and appearance will help you to protect your Body Image Vault and banish your Body Image Thief.

Have a go at answering the questions in the Body Image Box below to help you identify what your own body talk is like and how you can change this for the better.

BODY IMAGE BOX

What words do you currently use when talking about *your appearance* to other people?

....

....

What effects does this have on you?

....

....

How could you improve this aspect of your body talk?

....

....

What words do you currently use when talking about *the appearance of people you know?*

....

....

What effects does this have on you?

....

....

What effects does this have on them?

....

....

How could you improve this aspect of your body talk?

....

....

What words do you currently use when talking about *the appearance of celebrities?*

....

....

What effects does this have on you?

....

....

How could you improve this aspect of your body talk?

....

....

Having fun and enjoyment

It is important to ensure that you:

- get time for yourself every day
- give yourself things to look forward to
- increase your positive activity levels
- try new positive challenges
- have fun!

All of these will help you to realise that life doesn't have to be all about your concerns about your appearance! They will also give you the opportunity to feel more positive about yourself and your life and to banish your Body Image Thief!

It is also important to learn to have fun with appearance-related activities, such as going shopping or getting a hair cut. Do them because you choose to and you enjoy them, not because you feel you have to do them!

Q. Name one positive and enjoyable new activity you could add to your life and routine at the moment.

....

Being assertive

As human beings, we all have certain rights.

Q. List three rights you think you have as a human.

....
....
....

You may have written three of the following or you may have picked other rights which are just as valid:

- to be treated with respect
- to say 'No!'
- to have choice
- to be listened to
- to not be physically harmed by others
- to express your opinions
- to ask for help.

When you are assertive, you recognise that your rights are equal to those of other people and you respect your own rights and the rights of others. Thus, being assertive involves:

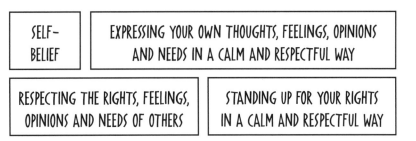

| SELF-BELIEF | EXPRESSING YOUR OWN THOUGHTS, FEELINGS, OPINIONS AND NEEDS IN A CALM AND RESPECTFUL WAY |
| RESPECTING THE RIGHTS, FEELINGS, OPINIONS AND NEEDS OF OTHERS | STANDING UP FOR YOUR RIGHTS IN A CALM AND RESPECTFUL WAY |

These assertiveness skills are helpful to improving your body image in a number of ways, including helping you to:

- say 'No!' in response to unrealistic pressures or demands that are influencing your body image concerns
- ask for help
- deal with people who are disrespectful to you in relation to your appearance
- deal with appearance-related bullying
- banish your Body Image Thief!

SAM'S STORY

Sam is 10 years old. He is being bullied by other boys at school. They say cruel things about him wearing glasses and being short and thin. They shout nasty names across the playground so other pupils can hear. And they also shout the names in the street as they take a similar route home from school as Sam. They have now started putting nasty things about how Sam looks on social networking sites.

Q. In what ways can Sam deal with this bullying assertively?

....

....

....

You may have written that Sam could:

- calmly and assertively tell the people who are bullying him that their actions make them look bad, not him

- tell a person he trusts about the bullying, such as a parent or teacher

- remember that even though everyone is entitled to their opinion it doesn't mean that the opinion is factual

- remember that he is entitled to be treated with respect

- remind himself of all the good things about him.

Living healthily

It is important that your goals in life involve achieving better health rather than losing weight or fixing certain body parts. Remember, the size of a person's body does not always reflect the health of their body. Every shape has the potential to be healthy if healthy eating and healthy exercise are part of a daily routine. So learn about the differences that good nutrition can make. Find a form of exercise that you enjoy doing and make it part of your regular routine but in a sensible way. And remember, food should be fun! Listen to your body and trust it to know when it is hungry and needs food and when it is full. Give your body enough rest too! All of this will help you to protect your Body Image Vault and banish your Body Image Thief!

It's time to do some of your own research again. Go online or look in books at the library in order to find out the answers to the questions in the next Body Image Box.

BODY IMAGE BOX

What does a healthy balanced diet involve?

....

....

....

....

....

What does a healthy amount of exercise involve?

....

....

....

....

....

What does a healthy amount of sleep involve?

....

....

....

....

....

Focusing your attention

Mindfulness teaches us that we have a choice as to what we focus our attention on in the here and now and that we can observe without making judgments. Learning how to do this more in everyday life can help us to overcome negative body image behaviours and to cope with situations more constructively – thus helping us to banish our Body Image Thief!

For example, if you find that you often compare your physical appearance to that of other people you meet, you need to instead focus your attention on the bigger picture. This can involve:

- paying attention to things about the person other than their appearance

- paying attention to the conversation you might be having with them or whatever other activity you are doing at the time

- paying attention to your surroundings using all your senses

...and doing all this without making any negative judgments or comparisons. Instead, just enjoy being in the moment! Practise this the next time you speak to someone.

You have learnt about managing your self-defeating behaviours and implementing constructive behaviours – all of which help to mend and protect your Body Image Vault and banish your Body Image Thief! Write down your own managing behaviours goals in the next Body Image Box.

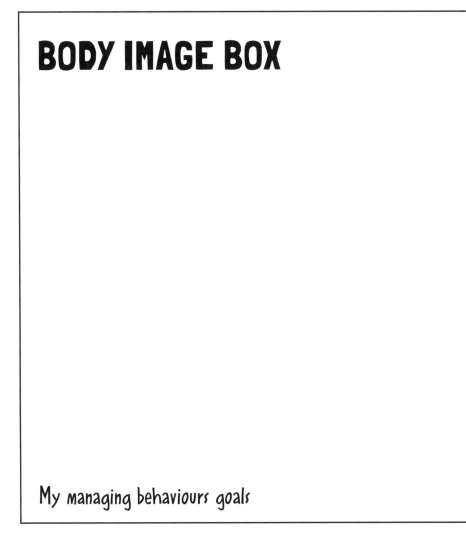

BODY IMAGE BOX

My managing behaviours goals

Good luck meeting these goals and banishing your Body Image Thief!

Body Image
Dos and Don'ts

Now it's time for you to think about everything you have learnt so far to help you to come up with your own personal list of Body Image Dos and Don'ts. Write at least five of each in the Body Image Box on the next page. Remember that the Dos will banish your Body Image Thief! Then write down the impacts that you think these Dos and Don'ts would have on you.

Some people find it helpful to carry this list around with them in their bag or to put a copy of it up on their wall at home so that they can look at it and remind themselves of what to do at times when they are finding their Body Image Thief difficult to banish!

BODY IMAGE BOX

DOS	DON'TS
IMPACTS	IMPACTS

Next is an example of a Dos and Don'ts list from Kaitlyn, aged 13 years.

BODY IMAGE BOX

DOS	DON'TS
Think realistically.	Place unrealistic expectations on myself and my appearance.
Realise that no-one is perfect.	Get angry with myself for not looking like the females in the magazines.
Realise that very few people can achieve the ideal body types.	Take my anger out on others.
Accept my looks and be happy with them.	Spend hours every day in front of the mirror fixing my hair and my make-up.
Reduce my excessive grooming behaviours.	Avoid situations because of how I look.
Stop comparing myself to the pictures I see in magazines.	Skip meals.
Start putting myself in situations that I would normally avoid because of my worries about how I look.	
Talk to my close friends about how I feel.	
Eat healthily.	
Exercise in moderation.	

IMPACTS	IMPACTS
I will feel better about how I look.	I will worry that I'm not perfect enough.
I will be more accepting of my flaws.	I will risk my health by skipping meals.
I will waste less time on things I don't need to do.	I will waste so much time on things I don't need to do.
I will have more time to do things I enjoy.	I will put strain on my relationships with others.
I will be able to do things I want to do without having to fear them because of my looks.	I will waste too much of my pocket money on make-up.
I will get on better with my friends and family.	I will miss out on doing things that I enjoy.
I will be healthier.	I will be unhappy.
I will be happier.	I will be worried.
My body image will be more positive.	I will be angry.
I will banish my Body Image Thief!	I will be sad.
	My body image will be negative.
	My Body Image Vault will be full of negativity!

Here's an example of a Dos and Don'ts list from Jonah, aged 16 years.

BODY IMAGE BOX

DOS

Develop more realistic deeper beliefs.
Realise that how I look isn't really that important.
Realise that I want to be fit in order to be healthy, not because I need to look a certain way.
Respond assertively if people make negative comments about my appearance.
Remember that it's the kind of person that I am that counts.
Eat healthy meals.
Stop taking steroids.
Stop drinking protein shakes.
Keep my exercise regime sensible.
Protect my Vault!

DON'TS

Take steroids.
Drink protein shakes.
Exercise to excess.
Spend hours in my room looking in the mirror.
Get angry when people make comments about my appearance.
Eat junk food because I'm sad about how I look.
Think in unrealistic ways.
Believe that I have to be muscular in order to be attractive.
Believe that looks are the only thing that is important when it comes to being happy and successful.
Let the Body Image Thief into my Vault!

IMPACTS

I will feel better about my body.
I will like me more.
I will have more realistic beliefs and thoughts.
I will be happier.
I will be healthier.
I will have a positive body image.
Life will be better.
I will have banished my Thief!

IMPACTS

I will feel miserable.
I will feel angry and frustrated.
I will feel alone and unloved.
I will be risking my health.
I will be overweight from overeating junk food.
I will get in trouble for getting aggressive towards people when I get angry.
I will have a negative body image.
I will have let the Thief into my Vault!

Summing Up!

We have now gone through all the methods you may need to banish your Body Image Thief and improve your body image. It's now down to you to put them all into practice. But don't forget you may not need them all. Just work on implementing those that are relevant to you and your body image.

REMEMBER...

Only YOU can change how you think and feel about your body!

Only YOU can change how you act

in response to those thoughts and feelings!

YOU'RE the one in control of your body image!

YOU have all the power to banish your Body Image Thief!

Let's have a quick recap before we finish.

Write down five things that you have learnt about your body image and how to improve it in the Body Image Box below.

BODY IMAGE BOX

What I have learnt

Let's also check what you have learnt by taking a Body Image Quiz!

THE BODY IMAGE QUIZ!

1. **Name the four main categories of negative body image-related behaviours.**

    1. ....

    2. ....

    3. ....

    4. ....

2. **Which of the following can have a potential influence on your behaviour? Tick your answers.**

    a) Difficult, stressful and traumatic life experiences ☐

    b) Your actual appearance ☐

    c) Your interactions with others ☐

    d) Societal messages ☐

3. **Name three types of thinking errors.**

    1. ....

    2. ....

    3. ....

4. **Unravel the word to find out who wants to steal your positive body image.**

    HET YODB AGEMI HIEFT

5. **Name two aspects of your life that a negative body image can affect.**

    1. ....

    2. ....

6. **Unravel this word to reveal a feeling that some people with a negative body image have about their bodies.**

    FACIONTSATDISSI

7. **Body image is how you _____ and feel about your body. What is the missing word? Tick which answers apply to you.**

    a) Ask ☐   c) Think ☐

    b) Tell ☐   d) Voice ☐

8. **What is the place where you can store your thoughts and feelings about your body image called? Tick which answers apply to you.**

    a) The Body Image Safe ☐

    b) The Body Image Safety Deposit Box ☐

    c) The Body Image Cave ☐

    d) The Body Image Vault ☐

9. **What do you need to do to your Body Image Thief? Tick which answers apply to you.**

    a) Hug him ☐   b) Banish him ☐

10. **Name three ways to help banish your Body Image Thief.**

    ....
    ....
    ....

Turn to the Appendix to see how you've got on!

Well done! I'm sure you did brilliantly!

Now have a go at advising two other young people on their body image issues, again to see just how much you have learnt about body image while working through this book.

BODY IMAGE AUNT OR UNCLE!
LETTER 1

Josie is 14 years old. She is so desperate to look like the women she sees on the TV and in magazines that she spends hours in front of the mirror every day poking and prodding at every part of her face to see if it has improved in any way as a result of all her efforts. She tries out new hairstyles that she sees on the celebrities that she admires in the hope that they will improve her face in some way. She applies different moisturisers, cleansers and toners over and over again in the hope that it will even out her complexion. And she spends all her pocket money every week on the latest make-up and beauty products, praying that this time one of them will work.

Josie is tall and slim. She can wear anything she likes as it always looks good on her body, but Josie hates her face. She would give anything to be able to have plastic surgery to rectify what she sees as a wonky nose, horrible bags under her eyes and red and blotchy skin. Her friends and family tell her all the time that her face is beautiful because Josie is always asking them how she looks, but she never believes them.

Josie has been finding it harder and harder to go out in public because of her worries about her face and last week she refused to go to school for the first time for a whole week. It's Sunday night and she already feels sick at the thought of having to go to school tomorrow and she has spent the whole day staring at her face in the mirror and trying to find new ways to disguise the flaws she sees.

Write down below the advice that you would give to Josie:

....
....
....
....
....
....
....
....
....
....

BODY IMAGE AUNT OR UNCLE!
LETTER 2

Matthew is 13 years old. His friends are all taller than him and they tease him a lot about his height, calling him names like 'titch', 'shortie' and 'the midget'. Matthew feels like a wimp in comparison to his friends because of his height. He is so worried that he will never be as tall as he wants to be because his dad is also 'too short' in Matthew's eyes at 5 foot 6 inches. Matthew is so afraid that he will never be a true 'man' unless he is tall.

Matthew's friends have started to date girls at school, but when Matthew asked out a girl he liked a few weeks ago, she turned him down. He is convinced it is because she thought he was too short and he believes that he will never get a girlfriend because of his height.

Matthew is devastated because he knows that there is nothing he can do to change his height and that makes him angry and down. He feels worthless and everything seems hopeless to him. He's stopped playing tennis because he feels humiliated when he is surrounded by taller players even though he has won so many youth competitions.

Write down below the advice that you would give to Matthew:

....
....
....
....
....
....
....
....
....

Now have a go at a more creative way of reinforcing what you have learnt with the following activity. If you wanted to spread the word far and wide to children and/or young people about body image and how it can be improved, what would you do? Pick whether you would:

- design a website for children and/or young people to access

- design a poster campaign for schools and/or colleges

- design scenes for an advert aimed at children and/or young people

- give a talk in schools and/or colleges

- deliver a play in schools and/or colleges.

Then in the box below, jot down ideas on the kinds of things you would include in whichever type of campaign method you would use. And if you want to have a go at completing your campaign advert, poster, website, etc. on some separate paper or on a computer, go ahead. Just think, maybe your school or college might want to use it!

TEACHING CHILDREN AND YOUNG PEOPLE ABOUT BODY IMAGE!

Let's get creative

Now let's check on how your body image has changed during the course of reading this book by re-taking the My Body Image Questionnaire. You will notice that there are now extra questions at the end! Have a go at answering the questions to see how well you've been banishing your Body Image Thief.

MY BODY IMAGE QUESTIONNAIRE

1. **How happy are you with your overall appearance? Tick which answer applies to you.**

   a) Very happy ☐   c) Mostly unhappy ☐

   b) Mostly happy ☐   d) Very unhappy ☐

2. **Do you worry a lot about your appearance? Tick which answer applies to you.**

   a) Yes ☐   b) No ☐

3. **At what age did you start to worry about your appearance? Tick which answer applies to you.**

   a) 0–5 years old ☐   c) 11–15 years old ☐

   b) 6–10 years old ☐   d) 16–18 years old ☐

4. **Do you wish that you could worry about your appearance less? Tick which answer applies to you.**

    a) Yes ☐   b) No ☐

5. **How different is how you look from how you would like to look? Tick which answer applies to you.**

    a) Completely different ☐   c) A little different ☐

    b) Quite a bit different ☐   d) No difference ☐

6. **Dotted around the skeleton below are different physical characteristics. Please colour in or highlight any that relate to parts of your body that you dislike. Then circle the ones that are causing you most concern, distress or worry at the moment.**

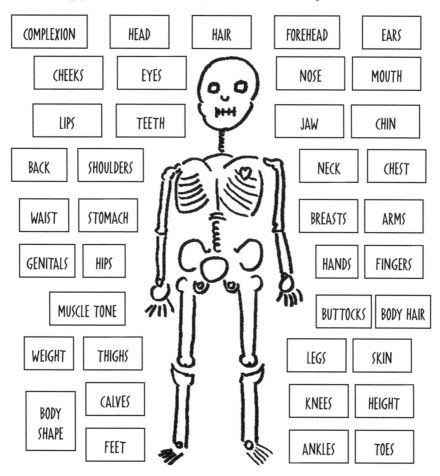

| COMPLEXION | HEAD | HAIR | FOREHEAD | EARS |

CHEEKS   EYES   NOSE   MOUTH

LIPS   TEETH   JAW   CHIN

BACK   SHOULDERS   NECK   CHEST

WAIST   STOMACH   BREASTS   ARMS

GENITALS   HIPS   HANDS   FINGERS

MUSCLE TONE   BUTTOCKS   BODY HAIR

WEIGHT   THIGHS   LEGS   SKIN

BODY SHAPE   CALVES   KNEES   HEIGHT

FEET   ANKLES   TOES

7. **If there are other physical characteristics that cause you concern, distress or worry which aren't listed above, please write them down below.**

    ....
    ....
    ....
    ....

8. **From your answers to questions 4 and 5, pick the parts of your physical appearance that cause you the most concern, distress or worry and write down below why you don't like them.**

    ....
    ....
    ....
    ....

9. **How noticeable do you think the physical characteristics that you don't like are to other people? Tick which answer applies to you.**

    a) Not at all   ☐   d) Very   ☐

    b) Slightly   ☐   e) Extremely   ☐

    c) Moderately   ☐

10. **How much time do you spend thinking about your appearance each day? Tick which answer applies to you.**

    a) Less than an hour per day   ☐

    b) 1 to 3 hours per day   ☐

    c) More than 3 hours and less than 8 hours a day   ☐

    d) More than 8 hours per day   ☐

11. In the table below is a list of different types of appearance-related thoughts that people can have. Please indicate in the table how often you have these types of thoughts.

TYPE OF THOUGHT	HOW OFTEN I HAVE THAT TYPE OF THOUGHT				
	VERY OFTEN	OFTEN	SOMETIMES	RARELY	NEVER
Other people treat me differently because of my appearance					
Other people think I am unattractive					
Other people stare at me, talk about me or laugh at me because of my appearance					
The first thing that people notice about me is what's wrong with my appearance					
I am unattractive					
I dislike the way I look					
If my appearance is not attractive enough, then I am a worthless person					
If my appearance is not attractive enough, then I will have no friends					

TYPE OF THOUGHT	HOW OFTEN I HAVE THAT TYPE OF THOUGHT				
	VERY OFTEN	OFTEN	SOMETIMES	RARELY	NEVER
If my appearance is not attractive enough, no-one will ever love me					
I must look perfect					
My appearance is an important part of who I am					
My appearance is more important in life than other things about me					
If I looked better, I would be happier					
If I looked better, my life would be better					
My appearance has ruined my life					
No-one will ever like me unless I change how I look					
I need to radically change how I look					
How you look on the outside is a sign of who you are on the inside					
Everyone else of a similar age to me looks better than me					

TYPE OF THOUGHT	HOW OFTEN I HAVE THAT TYPE OF THOUGHT				
	VERY OFTEN	OFTEN	SOMETIMES	RARELY	NEVER
If I didn't hide or camouflage how I really look, people wouldn't like me					
I have to look perfect for people to like me					
I will never look as attractive as others					
If my appearance is flawed, then I can't be attractive					
The only way to feel better is to change how I look					
I need to be thin to be attractive					
I need to be curvy to be attractive					
I need to be muscular to be attractive					
There is nothing I can do to look good					
People are only trying to make me feel better when they pay me compliments					

12. Do you regularly avoid any of the following because of your appearance? Highlight or colour in any that apply to you.

PUBLIC PLACES	SOCIAL SITUATIONS	BUYING NEW CLOTHES

LOOKING IN THE MIRROR OR OTHER REFLECTIVE SURFACES	PHYSICAL ACTIVITIES/SPORTS	PHYSICAL CONTACT WITH OTHERS

LOOKING AT YOURSELF WHEN UNDRESSED	DRESSING OR UNDRESSING IN FRONT OF OTHERS	HAVING YOUR PHOTOGRAPH TAKEN

BEING SEEN WITHOUT MAKE-UP	BEING SEEN IN BRIGHT LIGHTING OR FROM CERTAIN ANGLES	TRYING ON NEW CLOTHES AT THE SHOP

CONVERSATIONS ABOUT PHYSICAL APPEARANCE	BEING NEAR PEOPLE YOU THINK ARE ATTRACTIVE	LETTING PEOPLE SEE THE PARTS OF YOUR BODY YOU DISLIKE

OPPORTUNITIES FOR OTHER PEOPLE TO COMMENT ON YOUR APPEARANCE	OTHER BODY OR APPEARANCE-FOCUSED ACTIVITIES

13. Do you regularly use any of the following in order to 'hide' your appearance in some way? Highlight or colour in any that apply to you.

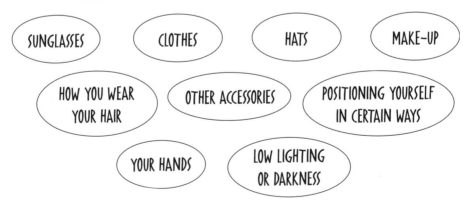

SUNGLASSES   CLOTHES   HATS   MAKE-UP

HOW YOU WEAR YOUR HAIR   OTHER ACCESSORIES   POSITIONING YOURSELF IN CERTAIN WAYS

YOUR HANDS   LOW LIGHTING OR DARKNESS

14. Do you do any of the following in order to try to 'fix' your appearance in some way? Highlight or colour in any that apply to you.

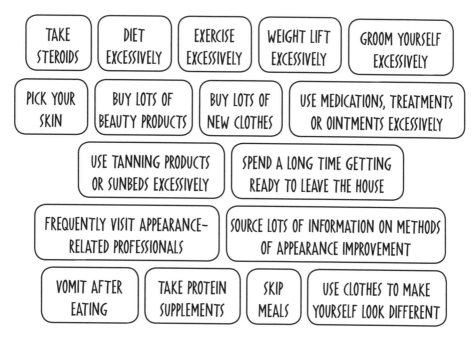

TAKE STEROIDS

DIET EXCESSIVELY

EXERCISE EXCESSIVELY

WEIGHT LIFT EXCESSIVELY

GROOM YOURSELF EXCESSIVELY

PICK YOUR SKIN

BUY LOTS OF BEAUTY PRODUCTS

BUY LOTS OF NEW CLOTHES

USE MEDICATIONS, TREATMENTS OR OINTMENTS EXCESSIVELY

USE TANNING PRODUCTS OR SUNBEDS EXCESSIVELY

SPEND A LONG TIME GETTING READY TO LEAVE THE HOUSE

FREQUENTLY VISIT APPEARANCE-RELATED PROFESSIONALS

SOURCE LOTS OF INFORMATION ON METHODS OF APPEARANCE IMPROVEMENT

VOMIT AFTER EATING

TAKE PROTEIN SUPPLEMENTS

SKIP MEALS

USE CLOTHES TO MAKE YOURSELF LOOK DIFFERENT

15. Have you ever had or thought about having cosmetic surgery or treatment because of your concerns about your appearance? Tick which answer applies to you.

a) Yes ☐   b) No ☐

16. Do you regularly do any of the following in order to 'check' your appearance in some way? Highlight or colour in any that apply to you.

SEEK REASSURANCE ABOUT HOW YOU LOOK FROM OTHERS

COMPARE YOURSELF TO OTHERS

CHECK YOUR APPEARANCE IN THE MIRROR

MEASURE PARTS OF YOUR BODY

CHECK YOUR BODY THROUGH TOUCHING, POKING, PRODDING, SQUEEZING, PINCHING AND PICKING

17. Do your appearance-related thoughts and behaviours cause you to feel any of the following? Highlight or colour in any that apply to you.

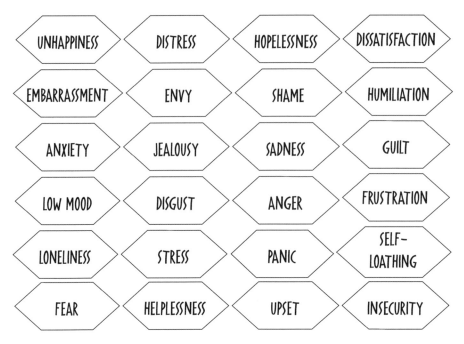

18. Has your body image had negative effects on any of the following aspects of your life? Highlight or colour in any that apply to you.

Physical health	Mental health and emotional wellbeing	Family relationships	Friendships

Performance at school/college/work/leisure activities	Motivation to do things	Romantic relationships

19. Do you believe changing your body image is in or out of your control? Tick which answer applies to you.

    a) In my control ☐   b) Out of my control ☐

20. Have you seen any changes in your body image since you completed the My Body Image Questionnaire at the start of the book? Tick which answer applies to you.

    a) Yes ☐   b) No ☐

21. If you have seen changes in your body image, what are they?

....

....

22. What goals would you like to set yourself so that you can continue to improve your ability to banish your Body Image Thief?

....

....

I hope that you have seen your body image become more positive and that you are changing the way in which you respond to your body for the better. As you continue to put everything you have learnt from this workbook into practice, occasionally ask yourself the questions from the My Body Image Questionnaire to monitor how far you have progressed and how well you're banishing your Body Image Thief! Also keep re-visiting the activities in the workbook to help you along the way.

But please be patient with yourself when putting all you've learnt into practice. You won't change everything overnight and, remember, no-one gets it right all the time. No-one is perfect!

And remember that you have to keep working on filling your Body Image Vault in positive and realistic ways and on protecting your Body Image Vault using constructive behaviours. This is especially important at times in your life when you are facing difficult life circumstances or you are feeling stressed or worried in some way, as these are the times when people are most susceptible to relapsing into negative body image again. These are the times when all of us are more likely to pop a few negative or unrealistic thoughts into our Vaults. These are also the times when all of us are more likely to act in self-defeating ways and thus blow a bulb in our Vault's security camera or weaken a hinge in our Vault door. But guess what?

Even if you have a temporary slip up, even if you throw a few negative thoughts about your body in your Vault and even if you avoid going to a party because you have a spot on your nose, thus blowing a bulb or weakening a hinge, it's not the end of the world!

Yes, OK, the Body Image Thief is a sneaky individual. He will be waiting around hoping for you to weaken your Vault's defence system in some way. He will be keeping his eyes peeled for a faulty lock or a loose chain in the hope that it's a sign of the whole defence system breaking down. This is because he wants you to let him back in again. He wants to steal all the positives from your Body Image Vault once more. But this does not mean that he can actually do this.

You see, one blown camera bulb does not equal a broken defence system as you still have all your other defences in place. And one blown camera bulb can be replaced with a new super-duper one that shines brighter than ever, keeping your Body Image Thief even further away from your Body Image Vault!

And don't forget, a few negative thoughts cannot take over your Body Image Vault unless YOU allow the Thief in to steal the positive ones, leaving plenty of space for the negative ones to multiply! And you have the power to push a few negative thoughts back into that dark, musty, dusty, cobwebby corner of the vault where they belong!

So even when times are difficult...

YOU are in control of your body image!

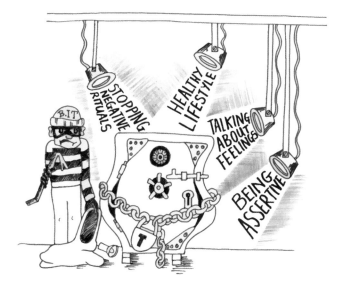

YOU can banish your Body Image Thief!

Just believe in YOU! Good luck!

This is to certify that

....

has successfully completed the
Banish Your Body Image Thief
workbook and can expertly

BANISH THEIR
BODY IMAGE THIEF!

APPENDIX

THE BODY IMAGE QUIZ ANSWERS

1. Avoidance, hiding, checking and fixing.
2. (a), (b), (c) and (d).
3. You may have included any of the thinking errors from the Body Image Box at the end of Chapter 6, such as magnification and catastrophising.
4. The Body Image Thief.
5. You may have listed any of the impacts discussed in Chapter 9, such as physical health and relationships.
6. Dissatisfaction.
7. (c) Think.
8. (d) The Body Image Vault.
9. (b) Banish him.
10. You may have included any of the 14 steps towards improving your body image given in Chapter 10, such as Step 1: Understanding what body image is. You may also have included any of the managing thoughts strategies from Chapter 11, such as realistic thinking, and any of the managing behaviours strategies from Chapter 12, such as graded exposure.

INFORMATION FOR PARENTS AND PROFESSIONALS

The purpose of this workbook

Banish Your Body Image Thief provides a cognitive behavioural and mindfulness approach to developing a positive body image for young people. It is designed for young people to work through on their own or with the support of a parent or a professional, such as a mental health practitioner, teacher, mentor, teaching assistant, social worker, doctor or youth worker.

This workbook has been designed for males and females aged 10 to 18 years who are experiencing varying levels of body image disturbance, including young people who are only mildly dissatisfied with their appearance, young people who are suffering body image disturbance as a result of an injury, wound, disfigurement or disability, young people suffering from the extreme body image dissatisfaction and associated distress and impairment that is indicative of body dysmorphic disorder (BDD) and young people suffering with an eating disorder that is related to body image issues.

However, it is important to note that although this workbook provides self-help tools that can be suitable for young people with varying levels of body image disturbance, it should not be considered to be a substitute for a diagnosis or treatment by a mental health professional where required, such as in the cases of BDD or eating disorders. Although research supports the use of a cognitive behavioural therapy approach for both BDD and eating disorders, studies also show that the complexity and severity of BDD and eating disorders can render the use of self-help resources alone as less effective than treatment managed by a mental health professional (e.g. Jarry and Ip 2005; Latner and Wilson 2007). However, *Banish Your Body Image Thief* can be used as an accompaniment to treatment with a professional in these types of cases for maximum benefit.

It is also imperative that young people seek immediate support from a mental health professional if they are experiencing depression, suicidal ideations or substance misuse as a result of or alongside their body image disturbance. In addition, it is also recommended that young people seek support from medical professionals if their body image issues have led to physical problems, such as those resulting from excessive exercise or dieting. Again, *Banish Your Body Image Thief* can be used as an accompaniment to treatment with a professional in these types of cases for maximum benefit.

The information provided within this workbook can also provide useful information for those individuals wishing to learn more about body image disturbance in order to help support a family member or friend.

Furthermore, although the self-help materials included in this workbook do not constitute a session-by-session therapeutic programme, they can be used as a useful resource for therapists working with young people. In this regard, it is important to note that the My Body Image Questionnaire in Chapter 2 is a tool for young people to explore and gain a better understanding of their own body image, but is not designed to be used as a clinical diagnostic tool.

Body image issues in children and young people

More and more research is being published every year on body image-related issues, and it is clear from the research that body image is a real concern for children and young people (e.g. Swami, Taylor and Carvalho 2011). The key areas that research has focused on have included: links between age and body image; gender differences in body image; influences on body image; and the behaviours and impacts associated with a negative body image.

Regarding age, studies indicate that, although body image issues are particularly prevalent in adolescence (e.g. Children's Society 2012; Etcoff *et al.* 2006; Ofsted 2008; Tremblay and Lariviere 2009; World Health Organization 2011), more and more young children are developing body image concerns in modern society too (e.g. Birbeck and Drummond 2006; Papadopoulos 2010; Schur *et al.* 2000). For example, Dohnt and Tiggemann (2006) reported that girls are becoming aware of beauty ideals and dieting methods as young as 5 to 8 years of age.

Regarding gender, the myth that body image issues are confined to girls is being dispelled, with an increasing amount of research highlighting how body image issues in young males is very much on the increase (e.g. Grogan and Richards 2002; Hargreaves and Tiggemann 2006; Hintikka *et al.* 2000). Studies looking at gender differences in relation to body image are finding that young females wish to be thinner, while young males wish to be more muscular (e.g. Ricciardelli *et al.* 2006, 2011).

Regarding influences, the key influences (both positive and negative) that repeatedly come up in studies, including for children and young people of both genders, include family members and peers (e.g. Cash, Rudiger and Williams 2008; Lowes and Tiggemann 2003; Tucker *et al.* 2007) as well as the societal, media (e.g. magazines, television, films, advertising) and fashion and beauty industry messages on 'ideal' body types that are unachievable for the majority of the population (e.g. Botta 2000; Dittmar 2009; Dohnt and Tiggeman 2006; Field *et al.* 2001; Harrison and Bond 2007; Knauss, Paxton and Alsaker 2007; Lorenzen, Grieve and Thomas 2004; Swami *et al.* 2011).

Regarding behaviours associated with negative body image, research continues to highlight the prevalence of behaviours such as avoidance of activities (e.g. Dove 2010; Etcoff *et al.* 2006), unhealthy weight control behaviours (e.g. Neumark-Sztainer 2005), steroid usage (e.g. Smith and Flatley 2011; YMCA, Centre for Appearance Research and the Succeed Foundation 2011), comparing self to others (e.g. Botta 2000) and accessing cosmetic surgery (e.g. Veale 2004; and the results of a 2011 body image survey by the Succeed Foundation).

Regarding the impacts of negative body image on children and young people, research has particularly focused on its consequences for health and wellbeing (APPG 2012) and the links with other mental health issues, such as depression (Sinton and Birch 2006) and eating disorders (Stice 2002), and with low self-esteem (APPG 2012).

Body image disturbance, body dysmorphic disorder, muscle dysmorphia and eating disorders

It is important to be aware that none of us will be content with every aspect of our appearance all the time, especially during adolescence, as the research discussed above highlights. However, although occasional and mild body image dissatisfaction with minimum impacts is common in children and young people, not all such appearance concerns are mild and fleeting. Sometimes they can be more severe and sometimes they can be indicative of a disorder known as BDD.

According to the 5th edition of the *Diagnostic and Statistical Manual of Mental Disorders* (DSM-V) (American Psychiatric Association 2013), BDD is the diagnosis given to an individual:

- who has a preoccupation with (i.e. thinks obsessively about) at least one perceived defect that doesn't exist or has a disproportionate concern over a slight physical defect (e.g. mild acne or a small scar)

- who performs repetitive behaviours (to check, improve or hide the perceived/minimal defect) or repetitive mental acts (such as comparing self to others) in response to the appearance concerns

- for whom the preoccupation causes significant distress, disrupts daily functioning or both

- whose symptoms are not better explained by diagnostic criteria for an eating disorder.

Sufferers are also divided for treatment purposes into those who:

- can acknowledge that their reaction to their perceived or minimal defect is inaccurate or out of proportion but don't know how to control their obsessive thoughts and compulsive behaviours (termed as having good or fair insight)

- think that their beliefs are probably true (termed as having poor insight)

- are completely convinced that their beliefs are true (termed as having absent insight or delusional beliefs).

BDD can relate to any part of the body, with many individuals having multiple concerns and some individuals being concerned about almost every aspect of how they look. Over time these concerns can either remain static, be added to with concerns over other body parts or completely change to concerns over different body parts. The type and severity of the BDD symptoms can vary from person to person and the condition can become chronic if left untreated. BDD is thought to affect males and females fairly equally and tends to develop during adolescence. Despite this, research on BDD in children and young people, including its presentation and prevalence, is limited. However, the research that is available shows its presentation to be similar to that in adults.

Muscle dysmorphia is a subtype of BDD that involves a preoccupation with muscularity, irrespective of actual muscle tone. This can often lead to compulsive exercise of a bodybuilding nature and, in some cases, the overuse of protein supplements and/or abuse of anabolic steroids.

Young people suffering from eating disorders, such as anorexia nervosa, bulimia nervosa and binge eating disorder, can also experience a preoccupation and dissatisfaction with their appearance and an unrealistic body image.

Anorexia nervosa is characterised by a relentless pursuit of thinness, a fear of weight gain and a perception of being overweight even when the individual is severely underweight. Weight-loss measures can include extreme exercise, extreme dieting, self-induced vomiting and/or the use of weight-loss pills, laxatives or enemas.

Bulimia nervosa involves frequent, recurrent episodes of eating unusually large amounts of food (binges), often in secret, followed by a compensatory behavioural response to the lack of control, guilt, self-loathing and fear of weight gain that can result from the binge. The compensatory behaviour may involve purging (such as self-induced vomiting or the excessive use of laxatives or diuretics), skipping meals and/or excessive exercise.

Binge eating disorder involves compulsive binge eating without efforts to purge or compensate for the binge.

Due to their symptoms, eating disorders create similarities with BDD sufferers. But at the same time, there are also differences. For example, whereas BDD commonly involves a preoccupation with one or more particular body feature, eating disorder sufferers are in the main more focused on concerns regarding overall body weight and shape. However, it is important to note that the distinction isn't always this clear cut and it can be argued that there is a grey area between the disorders. This can be complicated further by the fact that the same individual can suffer from both BDD and an eating disorder.

What is cognitive behavioural therapy (CBT)?

CBT is an evidence-based, skills-based, structured form of psychotherapy, which emerged from Beck's Cognitive Therapy (e.g. Beck 1976) and Ellis's Rational-Emotive Therapy (e.g. Ellis 1962), as well as from the work of behaviourists such as Pavlov (e.g. Pavlov 1927) and Skinner (e.g. Skinner 1938) on classical and operant conditioning respectively. CBT looks at the relationships between our thoughts (cognition), our feelings (emotions) and our actions (behaviours). It is based on the premise that how we interpret experiences and situations has a profound effect on our behaviours and emotions.

CBT focuses on:

- the problems that the client is experiencing in the here and now

- why the problems are occurring

- what strategies the client can use in order to address the problems.

The therapeutic process achieves this by empowering the client to identify:

- negative, unhealthy and unrealistic patterns of thoughts, perspectives and beliefs

- maladaptive and unhealthy patterns of behaviour

- the links between the problems the client is facing and his or her patterns of thoughts and behaviours

- how to challenge the existing patterns of thoughts and behaviours and implement alternative thoughts and behaviours that are constructive, healthy and realistic in order to address problems, manage emotions and improve wellbeing.

Thus the underlying ethos of CBT is that by addressing unhelpful patterns of thoughts and behaviours, people can change how they feel, how they view themselves, how they interact with others and how they approach life in general – thereby moving from an unhealthy cycle of reactions to a healthy one.

A wide range of empirical studies show CBT to be effective with many emotional wellbeing and mental health issues, including:

- body image disturbance and BDD (see following section for research details)

- anxiety (e.g. Cartwright-Hatton *et al.* 2004; James, Soler and Weatherall 2005)

- obsessive compulsive disorder (OCD) (e.g. O'Kearney *et al.* 2006)

- depression (e.g. Klein, Jacobs and Reinecke 2007).

CBT and body image

When addressing body image issues, CBT looks at modifying patterns of unhealthy appearance-related thoughts and beliefs as well as patterns of maladaptive behaviours, such as avoidance behaviours and appearance-related rituals, through techniques such as psychoeducation, cognitive restructuring, exposure and response prevention, perceptual mirror retraining and relapse prevention.

Research on interventions for body image disturbance and BDD is still very limited, with more extensive and up-to-date studies being required. However, CBT has become established as an effective treatment method for body image disturbance, with scholarly reviews of the limited empirical research available showing that CBT can lead to improvements in how people feel about their appearance (e.g. Hrabosky and Cash 2007; Jarry and Berardi 2004; Jarry and Ip 2005) and associated eating attitudes and behaviours (Jarry and Berardi 2004). The limited studies available also show CBT to be effective with BDD (e.g. Rosen, Reiter and Orosan 1995; Veale *et al*. 1996; Wilhelm *et al*. 2011) as well as with milder body image dissatisfaction and disturbance (e.g. Butters and Cash 1987). As a result, guidelines published by the National Institute for Clinical Excellence (NICE) recommend the use of CBT and self-help materials for adults and adolescents with BDD (NICE 2005).

CBT aimed at addressing body image issues has also been found to produce positive impacts upon other emotional wellbeing and mental health issues associated with body image disturbance, including anxiety, depression and low self-esteem (Jarry and Berardi 2004; Jarry and Ip 2005).

Effectiveness of CBT for children and young people

Although there has been less research conducted on the use of CBT with children and young people than there has been with adults, evidence for its effectiveness is continuing to grow and is being reported in a number of reviews, such as Kazdin and Weisz (1998) and Rapee *et al*. (2000). Extensive research is still required on CBT and other treatment options for body image disturbance and BDD in children and young people. However, random clinical trials have shown CBT to be effective with children and young people for:

- obsessive compulsive disorder (Barrett, Healy-Farrell and March 2004)
- depression (Lewinsohn and Clarke 1999)
- generalised anxiety disorder (Kendall *et al*. 1997, 2004)
- specific phobias (Silverman *et al*. 1999)
- social phobia (Spence, Donovan and Brechman-Toussaint 2000)
- school refusal (King *et al*. 1998).

What is mindfulness?

Mindfulness originates from spiritual disciplines such as Buddhism and from practices such as meditation and yoga. The essence of mindfulness is that we can make a choice to:

- focus our attention on the present moment, thus engaging fully in the here and now with all our senses

- accept our thoughts and feelings as they are, thus observing them without criticism or judgment

- let those thoughts and feelings go, thus reducing any negative impact.

In the 1970s, mindfulness principles and practices were incorporated into a form of training known as mindfulness-based stress reduction (MBSR) developed by Jon Kabat-Zinn. In the 1990s, principles of mindfulness also emerged within psychotherapy and became known as Mindfulness-Based Cognitive Therapy (MBCT) for use with people with a history of depression.

The key principles of mindfulness detailed above are also now incorporated into Acceptance and Commitment Therapy (ACT), a mindfulness and values-based form of behavioural therapy. ACT sees our 'private experiences' (namely our thoughts, feelings and physical sensations) as not harmful in themselves. What is seen as harmful within ACT is how we choose to respond to those private experiences, such as seeing them as reality (what ACT terms 'cognitive fusion') and avoiding experiencing these thoughts, feelings and physical sensations (known as experiential avoidance). Thus, as well as teaching us principles of acceptance and being fully present in the moment, ACT also teaches us to make a distinction between our 'private experiences' and reality (a process known as 'cognitive defusion') and to commit to action which enriches and nourishes our lives based upon our values (known as values-consistent behaviours).

The empirical support for ACT as an effective form of treatment for mental health issues such as anxiety and depression is growing (e.g. Forman *et al.* 2007), and initial studies looking at its effectiveness for body image dissatisfaction are also showing positive impacts (e.g. Pearson, Follette and Hayes 2012).

Effectiveness of mindfulness-based therapies for children and young people

Research on the use of mindfulness-based therapies with children and young people is still in its infancy. However, evidence supporting its use is growing, especially in relation to ACT (e.g. Greco *et al.* 2005; Murrell and Scherbarth 2006). Studies are showing support for the use of ACT for children and young people with depression (Hayes, Boyd and Sewell 2011), generalised anxiety disorder (Greco 2002), anorexia nervosa (Heffner, Sperry and Eifert 2002) and pain (Greco *et al.* under review). And research is beginning to highlight how ACT can help to address the links between body image concerns and disordered eating in young people (Greco and Blomquist 2006).

REFERENCES

ACMD (2011) *ACMD Anabolic Steroids Advice*. London: Advisory Council on the Misuse of Drugs. Available at: www.gov.uk/government/publications/acmd-anabolic-steroids-advice-2011, accessed 1 November 2013.

American Psychiatric Association (2013) *Diagnostic and Statistical Manual of Mental Disorders*, DSM-V, 5th edition. Arlington, VA: American Psychiatric Publishing.

APPG (2012) *Reflections on Body Image*. London: All Party Parliamentary Group on Body Image and Central YMCA. Available at: www.ncb.org.uk/media/981233/appg_body_image_final.pdf, accessed 13 January 2014.

Association of Teachers and Lecturers (2013) 'Perfect bodies.' *Report Magazine*, June/July 2013. Available at: www.atl.org.uk/publications-and-resources/report/2013/2013-june-july-body-image.asp, accessed 12 November 2013.

Barrett, P., Healy-Farrell, L. and March, J.S. (2004) 'Cognitive-behavioural family treatment of childhood obsessive compulsive disorder: A controlled trial.' *Journal of the American Academy of Child and Adolescent Psychiatry 43*, 1, 46–62.

BBC Radio 1 Newsbeat and 1Xtra TXU survey (2007) Available at: www.bbc.co.uk/pressoffice/pressreleases/stories/2007/02_february/20/body.shtml, accessed 1 November 2013.

Beck, A.T. (1976) *Cognitive Therapy and Emotional Disorders*. New York: International Universities Press.

Birbeck, D. and Drummond, M. (2006) 'Very young children's body image: Bodies and minds under construction.' *International Education Journal 7*, 4, 423–434.

Bliss Magazine (2004) 'UK teen body image survey.' London: EMAP Consumer Media.

Botta, R.A. (2000) 'The mirror of television: A comparison of Black and White adolescents' body image.' *Journal of Communication 50*, 3, 144–159.

Bullying Online (2006) *The National Survey 2006: The Results*. Available at: http://parentingtt.files.wordpress.com/2011/05/thenationalbullyingsurvey_results.pdf, accessed 1 November 2013.

Butters, J.W. and Cash, T.F. (1987) 'Cognitive-behavioural treatment of women's body-image dissatisfaction.' *Journal of Consulting and Clinical Psychology 55*, 6, 889–897.

Cartwright-Hatton, S., Roberts, C., Chitsabesan, P., *et al.* (2004) 'Systematic review of the efficacy of cognitive behaviour therapies for childhood and adolescent anxiety disorders.' *British Journal of Clinical Psychology 43*, 4, 421–436.

Cash, T.F., Rudiger, J.A. and Williams, E.F. (2008) 'Protective factors in positive body image development: A qualitative study.' Quoted in T.F. Cash (2008) *The Body Image Workbook*, 2nd edition. Oakland, CA: New Harbinger Publications.

Centre for Appearance Research, 2012 survey, as cited in APPG (2012) *Reflections on Body Image*. London: All Party Parliamentary Group on Body Image and Central YMCA. Available at: www.ncb.org.uk/media/861233/appg_body_image_final.pdf, accessed 13 Janary 2014.

Centre for Appearance Research and the Central YMCA survey (2011) Reported at www.ymca.co.uk/bodyimage/sites/ymca.ndpclient.com.body-confidence/files/users/Body%20Confidence%20Selected%20Pages.pdf, accessed 1 November 2013.

Children's Society (2012) *The Good Childhood Inquiry Report 2012*. London: Children's Society. Available at: www.childrenssociety.org.uk/sites/default/files/tcs/good_childhood_report_2012_final_0.pdf, accessed 1 November 2013.

Credos (2011) *Pretty as a Picture*. London: Credos. Available at: www.credos.org.uk/write/Documents/Pretty%20as%20a%20picture%20Dec%2011.pdf, accessed 1 November 2013.

Dittmar, H. (2009) 'How do "body perfect" ideals in the media have a negative impact on body image and behaviors? Factors and processes related to self and identity.' *Journal of Social and Clinical Psychology 28*. (Special Issue: Body Image and Eating Disorders), 1–8.

Dohnt, H.K. and Tiggemann, M. (2006) 'Body image concerns in girls: The role of peers and media prior to adolescence.' *Journal of Youth and Adolescence 25*, 5, 615–630.

Dove (2010) *The Real Truth About Beauty Revisited: Dove Global Study 2010*, Unilever plc. Cited in Dove Self-Esteem Activity Guide: For Mothers and Daughters Aged 8–11, Dove Self-Esteem Project, Unilever UK. Available at: www.dove.co.uk/en/docs/pdf/Activity_Guide_for_Mothers_Daugthers_8_11.pdf, accessed 13 January 2014.

Eisenberg, M.E., Wall, M. and Neumark-Sztainer, D. (2012) 'Muscle-enhancing behaviors among adolescent girls and boys.' *Pediatrics 130*, 6, 1019–1026; originally published online 19 November 2012; doi: 10.1542/peds.2012-0095.

Ellis, A. (1962) *Reason and Emotion in Psychotherapy*. New York: Lyle-Stuart.

Etcoff, N., Orbach, S., Scott, J. and D'Agostino, H. (2006) *Beyond Stereotypes: Rebuilding the Foundation of Beauty Beliefs*. Findings of the 2005 Dove Global Study, Dove, Unilever plc. Available at: www.vawpreventionscotland.org.uk/sites/default/files/Dove%20Beyond%20Stereotypes%20White%20Paper.pdf, accessed 13 January 2014.

Field, A.E., Carmargo, C.A. Jr., Taylor, C.B., Berkeley, C.S., Roberts, S.B. and Colditz, G.A. (2001) 'Peer, parent and media influences on the development of weight concerns and frequent dieting among preadolescent and adolescent girls and boys.' *Pediatrics 107*, 1, 54–60.

Forman, E.M., Hoffman, K.L., McGrath, K.B., Herbert, J.D., Brandsma, L.L. and Lowe, M.R. (2007) 'A comparison of acceptance- and control-based strategies for coping with food cravings: An analog study.' *Behaviour Research and Therapy 45*, 1, 2372–2386.

Girl Guiding UK (2012) Survey results. Reported at http://girlsattitudes. girlguiding.org.uk/pdf/Girls%20Attitudes%202012%20results_Family%20 and%20relationships.pdf, accessed 13 January 2014.

Grazia Magazine (2006) 'Female Body Survey of Great Britain.' London: Grazia Magazine.

Greco (2002) 'Creating a context of acceptance in child clinical and paediatric settings.' Paper presented at the annual meeting of the Association for the Advancement of Behavior Therapy, Reno, NV.

Greco, L.A. and Blomquist, K.K. (2006) 'Body Image, Eating Behaviour, and Quality of Life among Adolescent Girls: Role of Anxiety and Acceptance Processes in a School Sample.' In K.S. Berlin and A.R. Murrell (Co-chairs) *Extending Acceptance and Mindfulness Research to Parents, Families and Adolescents: Process, Empirical Findings, Clinical Implications and Future Directions*. Symposium conducted at the Association for Behavior and Cognitive Therapies, Chicago, IL.

Greco, L.A., Blackledge, J.T., Coyne, L.W. and Ehrenreich, J. (2005) 'Integrating Acceptance and Mindfulness into Treatments for Child and Adolescent Anxiety Disorders: Acceptance and Commitment Therapy as an Example.' In S.M. Orsillo and L. Roemer (eds) *Acceptance and Mindfulness-Based Approaches to Anxiety: Conceptualization and Treatment*. New York: Springer Science.

Greco, L.A., Blomquist, K.K., Acra, S. and Moulton, D. (under review) 'Acceptance and commitment therapy for adolescents with functional abdominal pain: Results of a pilot investigation.' Manuscript submitted for publication. As cited in L. A. Greco and S.C. Hayes (2008) *Acceptance and Mindfulness Treatments for Children and Adolescents: A Practitioner's Guide*. Oakland, CA: New Harbinger Publications.

Grogan, S. and Richards, H. (2002) 'Body image: Focus groups with boys and men' *Men and Masculinities 4*, 3, 219–232.

Hargreaves, D.A. and Tiggemann, M. (2006) '"Body Image is for Girls": A qualitative study of boys' body image.' *Journal of Health Psychology 11*, 4, 567–576.

Harrison, K. and Bond, B.J. (2007) 'Gaming magazines and the drive for muscularity in preadolescent boys: A longitudinal examination.' *Body Image 4*, 3, 269–277.

Hayes, L., Boyd, C.P. and Sewell, J. (2011) 'Acceptance and Commitment Therapy for the treatment of adolescent depression: A pilot study in a psychiatric outpatient setting.' *Mindfulness 2*, 2, 86–94.

Heffner, M., Sperry, J. and Eifert, G.H. (2002) 'Acceptance and commitment therapy in the treatment of an adolescent female with anorexia nervosa: A case example.' *Cognitive and Behavioural Practice 9*, 3, 232–236.

Hintikka, J., Hintilla, U., Lehtonen, J., Viinamaki, H., Koskela, K. and Kontula, O. (2000) 'Sociocultural influences on body image and body change methods.' *Journal of Adolescent Health 26*, 1, 3–4.

Hrabosky, J.I. and Cash, T.F. (2007) 'Self-Help Treatment for Body Image Disturbances.' In J.D. Latner and G.T. Wilson (eds) *Self-Help Approaches for Obesity and Eating Disorders*. New York: Guilford Press.

James, A.A.C.J., Soler, A. and Weatherall, R.R.W. (2005) 'Cognitive behavioural therapy for anxiety disorders in children and adolescents.' *Cochrane Database of Systematic Reviews 2005*, Issue 4. Art. No.: CD004690. doi:10.1002/14651858.CD004690.pub2. Published online January 2009.

Jarry, J.L. and Berardi, K. (2004) 'Characteristics and effectiveness of stand-alone body image therapy: A review of the empirical literature.' *Body Image: An International Journal of Research 1*, 4, 319–333.

Jarry, J.L. and Ip, K. (2005) 'The effectiveness of stand-alone cognitive-behavioural therapy for body image: A meta-analysis.' *Body Image: An International Journal of Research 2*, 4, 317–331.

Kazdin, A.E. and Weisz, J.R. (1998) 'Identifying and developing empirically supported child and adolescent treatments.' *Journal of Consulting and Clinical Psychology 66*, 1, 19–36.

Kendall, P.C., Flannery-Schroeder, E., Panichelli-Mindel, S.M., Sotham-Gerow, M., Henin, A. and Warman, M. (1997) 'Therapy with youths with anxiety disorders: A second randomized clinical trial.' *Journal of Consulting and Clinical Psychology 65*, 3, 366–380.

Kendall, P.C., Safford, S., Flannery-Schroeder, E. and Webb, A. (2004) 'Child anxiety treatment: Outcomes in adolescence and impact on substance abuse and depression at 7.4 year follow-up.' *Journal of Consulting and Clinical Psychology 72*, 2, 276–287.

King, N.J., Molloy, G.N., Heyme, D., Murphy, G.C. and Ollendick, T. (1998) 'Emotive imagery treatment for childhood phobias: A credible and empirically validated intervention?' *Behavioural and Cognitive Psychotherapy 26*, 2, 103–113.

Klein, J.B., Jacobs, R.H. and Reinecke, M.A. (2007) 'Cognitive-behavioral therapy for adolescent depression: A meta-analytic investigation of changes in effect-size estimates.' *Journal of the American Academy of Child and Adolescent Psychiatry 46*, 11, 1403–1413.

Knauss, C., Paxton, S. and Alsaker, F.D. (2007) 'Relationships amongst body dissatisfaction internalization of the media body ideal and perceived pressure from media in adolescent boys and girls.' *Body Image 4*, 4, 353–360.

Latner, J.D., and Wilson, G.T. (2007) 'Continuing Care and Self-Help in the Treatment of Obesity.' In J.D. Latner and G.T. Wilson (eds) *Self-help Approaches for Obesity and Eating Disorders: Research and Practice*. New York: Guilford Press.

Lewinsohn, P.M. and Clarke, G.N. (1999) 'Psychosocial treatments for adolescent depression.' *Clinical Psychology Review 19*, 3, 329–342.

Lorenzen, L.A., Grieve, F.G. and Thomas, A. (2004) 'Exposure to muscular male models decreases men's body satisfaction.' *Sex Roles 51*, 11–12, 743–748.

Lowes, J. and Tiggemann, M. (2003) 'Body dissatisfaction, dieting awareness and the impact of parental influence in young children.' *British Journal of Health Psychology 8*, 2, 135–147.

Mission Australia (2010) *National Survey of Young Australians 2010*. Sydney: Mission Australia. Available at: www.missionaustralia.com.au/research-page/young-people-page, accessed 1 November 2013.

MORI (2012) *MORI Poll for International Women's Day 2012*. London: MORI.

Murrell, A.R., and Scherbarth, A.J. (2006) 'State of the research and literature address: ACT with children, adolescents and parents.' *International Journal of Behavioral Consultation and Therapy 2*, 4, 531–543.

Neumark-Sztainer, D. (2005) *'I'm Like So Fat!' Helping Your Teen Make Healthy Choices about Eating and Exercise in a Weight-Obsessed World*. New York: Guilford Press.

NICE (National Institute for Clinical Excellence) (2005) 'Obsessive compulsive disorder: Core interventions in the treatment of obsessive compulsive disorder and body dysmorphic disorder.' *Clinical Guideline 31*. Available at: www.nice.org.uk/nicemedia/pdf/CG031niceguideline.pdf, accessed 2 January 2012.

O'Connell, A. and Martin, S. (2012) *How We See It: Report of a Survey on Young People's Body Image*. Dublin: Department of Children and Youth Affairs, Government Publications. Available at: http://cdn.thejournal.ie/media/2012/10/dcya_bodyimage_final_01-1.pdf, accessed 13 January 2014.

O'Kearney, R.T., Anstey, K., von Sanden, C. and Hunt, A. (2006) 'Behavioural and cognitive behavioural therapy for obsessive compulsive disorder in children and adolescents.' *Cochrane Database of Systematic Reviews 2006*, Issue 4. Art. No.: CD004856. doi: 10.1002/14651858.CD004856. pub2. Published online January 2010.

Ofsted (2008) *Tellus 3: A Survey of the Views of Children and Young People*. London: The Office for Standards in Education. Available at: www.ofsted. gov.uk/resources/tellus-3-survey-of-views-of-children-and-young-people, accessed 1 November 2013.

Papadopoulos, L. (2010) *Sexualisation of Young People Review*. London: Home Office. Available at: http://webarchive.nationalarchives.gov.uk/+/http:/www.homeoffice.gov.uk/documents/Sexualisation-of-young-people2835.pdf?view=Binary, accessed 13 January 2014.

Pavlov, I.P. (1927) *Conditioned Reflexes: An Investigation of the Physiological Activity of the Cerebral Cortex.* Translated and edited by G.V. Anrep. Oxford: Oxford University Press.

Pearson, A., Follette, V.M. and Hayes, S.C. (2012) 'A pilot study of Acceptance and Commitment Therapy as a workshop intervention for body image dissatisfaction and disordered eating attitudes.' *Cognitive and Behavioral Practice 19*, 1, 181–197.

Rapee, R.M., Wignall, A., Hudson, J.L. and Schniering, C.A. (2000) *Treating Anxious Children and Adolescents: An Evidence-Based Approach.* Oakland, CA: New Harbinger Publications.

Ricciardelli, L.A., McCabe, M.D., Lillis, J. and Thomas, K. (2006) 'A longitudinal investigation of the development of weight and muscle concerns among preadolescent boys.' *Journal of Youth and Adolescence 35*, 2, 168–178.

Ricciardelli, L.A., Holt, K.E., Grogan, S. and McCabe, M.P. (2011) *The Role of Social Comparisons in Children's Body Image Concerns.* Deakin University (unpublished).

Rosen, J.C., Reiter, J. and Orosan, P. (1995) 'Cognitive behavior therapy for negative body image.' *Behaviour Therapy 20*, 3, 393–404.

Schur, E.A., Sanders, M. and Steiner, H. (2000) 'Body dissatisfaction and dieting in young children.' *International Journal of Eating Disorders 27*, 1, 74–82.

Silverman, W.K., Kurtines, W.M., Ginsburg, G.S., Weems, C.F., Rabian, B. and Setafini, L.T. (1999) 'Contingency management, self-control and education support in the treatment of childhood phobic disorders: A randomized clinical trial.' *Journal of Consulting and Clinical Psychology 67*, 5, 675–687.

Sinton, M. and Birch, L. (2006) 'Individual and sociocultural influences on pre-adolescent girls' schemas and body dissatisfaction.' *Journal of Youth and Adolescence 35*, 2, 165–175.

Skinner, B.F. (1938) *The Behavior of Organisms.* New York: Appleton-Century-Crofts.

Smith, K. and Flatley, J. (2011) 'Drug misuse declared: Findings from the 2010/11 British Crime Survey.' *Home Office Statistical Bulletin.* London: Home Office.

Spence, S., Donovan, C. and Brechman-Toussaint, M. (2000) 'The treatment of childhood social phobia: The effectiveness of a social skills training-based cognitive behavioural intervention with and without parental involvement.' *Journal of Child Psychology and Psychiatry 41*, 6, 713–726.

Stice, E. (2002) 'Body Image and Bulimia Nervosa.' In T.F. Cash and T Pruzinsky (eds) *Body Image: A Handbook of Theory, Research and Clinical Practice.* New York: Guilford Press.

Succeed Foundation Body Image Survey (2011). Results reported at http://info.uwe.ac.uk/news/UWENews/news.aspx?id=1949, accessed 12 November 2013.

Swami, V., Taylor, R. and Carvalho, C. (2011) 'Body dissatisfaction assessed by the Photographic Figure Rating Scale is associated with sociocultural, personality and media influences.' *Scandinavian Journal of Psychology* 52, 1, 57–63.

Tremblay, L. and Lariviere, M. (2009) 'The influence of puberty onset, body mass index and pressure to be thin on disordered eating behaviours in children and adolescents.' *Eating Behaviours 10*, 2, 75–83.

Tucker, K.L., Martz, D.M., Curtin, L.A. and Bazzini, B.G. (2007) 'Examining "fat talk" experimentally in a female dyad: How are women influenced by another woman's body presentation style?' *Body Image: An International Journal of Research 4*, 2, 157–164.

Veale, D. (2004) 'Advances in a cognitive behavioural model of body dysmorphic disorder.' *Body Image: An International Journal of Research 1*, 1, 113–125.

Veale, D., Boocock, A., Gournay, K., Dryden, W. *et al.* (1996) 'Body dysmorphic disorder: A survey of fifty cases.' *The British Journal of Psychiatry 169*, 1, 196–201.

Victoria University of Wellington's Youth Connectedness Survey (2007) Reported in *Youth Statistics: A Statistical Profile of Young People in New Zealand*, New Zealand's Ministry of Youth Development. Available at: www.youthstats.myd.govt.nz/indicator/happy-and-confident/body-image/index.html, accessed 1 November 2013.

Wilhelm, S., Phillips, K.A., Fama, J.M., Greenberg, J.L. and Steketee, G. (2011) 'Modular cognitive behavioural therapy for body dysmorphic disorder.' *Behaviour Therapy 42*, 4, 624–633.

World Health Organization (2011) *HBSC England National Report: Health Behaviour in School Children (HBSC)*. World Health Organization Collaborative Cross National Study. Hatfield: University of Hertfordshire.

YMCA (2011) *What do Politicians Think About Body Image Issues?* COMRES Poll. Available at: www.ymca.co.uk/body-confidence/sites/ymca.ndpclient.com.body-confidence/files/users/Parliament.pdf, accessed 1 November 2013.

YMCA, Centre for Appearance Research and the Succeed Foundation (2011) *Male BodyTalk*. Reported at www.ymca.co.uk/bodyimage/campaign/men, accessed 13 January 2014.

Young NCB NI Advisory Group and NCB NI Staff (2012) *My Body and I: Exploring How Young People in Northern Ireland Feel about their Body Image*. Available at: www.ncb.org.uk/media/820552/local_example-young_ncb_body_image_report_2012.pdf, accessed 1 November 2013.